Lives in Cricket: No 1

C000129741

Allan Watkins
A true all-rounder

Douglas Miller

With a foreword by Don Shepherd

First published in Great Britain by
Association of Cricket Statisticians and Historians
Cardiff CF11 9XR

© ACS, 2007

British Library Cataloguing-in-Publication Data.

A catalogue record for this book is available from the British
Library.

ISBN: 978 1 905138 46 3

Typeset by Limlow Books

Contents

Foreword
By Don Shepherd

Career statistics clearly demonstrate that Allan Watkins was a genuine all-round cricketer, highly skilled in three disciplines – batting, bowling and fielding; a man who served Glamorgan and England proudly to the best of his considerable ability. He should have received more than 15 caps for his country.

Left-handed in all things, Allan presented a reassuring presence as a middle-order batsman, steady and strong with temperament to fight the battle in adverse circumstances or attack with relish in pursuit of victory. Strong off the back foot with powerful pulls and square cuts, as many bowlers of the time will testify.

From a lengthy curving approach Allan was able to bowl swing and seam or left-arm spin as the conditions necessitated. Regularly the ball passed the right-hander's outside edge to bring forth a wry smile. No question of 'sledging'.

In an age of wonderful specialist close fielders, he was outstanding. Mostly stationed at leg slip he was a constant threat, able to catch off the inside edge or off genuine strokes.

Many bowlers, including myself, have much to thank him for. I clearly recall a startling diving catch to dismiss that fine player John Langridge from my bowling. On a wet Cardiff Arms Park surface, during my early days of pace bowling, we were able to measure his 'skid' marks - from take off to completion approximately 11 feet. Quite amazing.

Cricketing days over, Allan became a much respected coach at Christ College, Brecon; and then at Framlingham and Oundle. My private thoughts were that he might return to Glamorgan as senior coach. Alas, it wasn't to be. More's the pity.

Allan Watkins was a great team-mate, a wonderful cricketer, a family man and a friend to all who shared his company. One of Wales' great sportsmen.

Introduction

I first met Allan Watkins when I was asked to write a book on Don Shepherd. As I set out to see those who had played with Don, my first port of call had been Jim McConnon, whom I met just months before his death. Delightful man as Jim was, I had found his observations on cricket locked in the past. It was almost as though he had not noticed that the game had moved on into the commercial age of coloured clothing and third umpires.

How different it was when I called to see Allan Watkins a few weeks later. At his Oundle home, with his wife of sixty years beside him and chipping in freely, the conversation never flagged for three hours. Here was a man with the sharpest of memories and a perceptive eye for the deficiencies of the modern game. I soon discovered, too, that Allan has a gift for language – the spicy phrase that brings recollections to life and allows emotions to shine through.

When the idea was floated that the ACS should introduce a series of short biographies of cricketers whose deeds had not been previously chronicled, I wasted no time in lifting the telephone to Allan Watkins. He is, after all, a considerable cricketer with 20,361 first-class runs, 833 wickets and 461 catches. In the 1950s, of England-qualified players, only Trevor Bailey could lay serious claim to a better all-round record; and there was certainly a period when Allan's performances were superior to those of the man who was cemented into the England team. With 15 Test caps, perhaps fewer than he merited, Allan's story deserves to be more widely told.

I was delighted that Allan immediately agreed to co-operate with the project. Sadly, by 2006, he was a widower, so the occasional asides that find their way into the book from his devoted Molly have come from my earlier visit to the Watkins' home. It has been a huge pleasure to sit and listen to Allan drawing on his long and vivid memory of a life with the humblest of origins that became, through cricket, one of rich fulfilment. Allan's has been a life with few regrets, but it has not been free from moments of anguish and self-doubt, and I have felt very privileged to be allowed to hear of the inner turmoils that have afflicted him.

Douglas Miller, May 2007

Chapter One
Early Days at Usk

"Now before you go, Albert, you will get the kindling ready for the fire in the morning. And don't forget!" "Albert, before you go, you will go and turn those potatoes over."

Allan Watkins still remembers how his baptismal name, only discarded when he entered the first-class game, so often prefaced his father's attempts to impose some discipline on a young son bent only on an early escape to the cricket field.

Albert John Watkins was born on 21 April 1922 at Usk in Monmouthshire. The second of Jack and Mary Watkins' five children and the older of their two sons, it was as Albert that he travelled through childhood and into early adult life. The change to Allan came when, as an aspiring Glamorgan cricketer, he became the target of autograph hunters. "I wish I had a shorter

The Mill Street cottage (second door from the right) where Allan spent his childhood

name," he had said casually one day. "Why don't you sign as Allan?" his future skipper Wilfred Wooller suggested. So Allan did just that, curiously, and for no reason of which he is now aware, choosing to spell his adopted name with a double 'l'. So it was as Allan Watkins that some of the earliest press reports introduced him to the cricket world, though for most of those from around Usk he would remain Albert.

Jack Watkins

Once a bustling market town now tinged with the gentility of boutiques, Usk lays claim to be Britain's oldest continuously inhabited Roman settlement, tracing its history back to 55 AD. Allan's birthplace was in Old Market Street, but before long the family moved to 29 Mill Street, a modest terraced cottage on the outer edge of the town. All the cottages in the terrace are long demolished, and with them has

Mary Watkins

gone the wide open street that served, in car-free days, as a cricket and football pitch for the youngsters. Now, on both sides of the road, are semi-detached family homes, all with driveways; but the Watkins have not deserted Mill Street, for one of the new houses is home to Allan's brother Selwyn and his wife.

One of the joys of Allan's childhood was that Usk Cricket Club was no more than 40 yards from the family home. There is a new pavilion now, but the field with its broad boundaries remains, still catering for tennis, now with impressive floodlights, though it is no longer home to the once popular bowls club. Across the meadow just beyond the cricket field flows the river that shares its name with the town, seldom as high or as fast as it once was, though still bringing an occasional threat of flooding to the lower-lying buildings in the centre of the town.

Times were hard in the 1930s. Jack Watkins found what work he could as a labourer, while Mary spent most of her time caring for the children, supplementing the family income by helping out in local shops. But however stretched the purse, there was always good food on the table as Jack made the most of the large garden behind the cottage. "He was always out in his garden," says Allan. "It was an absolute joy – with everything in lines." Jack's green fingers ensured a constant supply of vegetables, while there was more work for the children helping to feed the chickens, ducks and pigs.

The five children.
From left: Selwyn, Millie, Sylvia, Allan, Dorothy

In later years, when the war brought rationing and shortages, Selwyn, nearly ten years Allan's junior and the self-confessed rebel of the pair, did his bit to keep the family self-sufficient with some discreet poaching by the river. "I've caught salmon with my bare hands," he says. "And rabbits – wait to see which way the farmer was going and then poach the rabbits!" Allan in his time had also poached a few fish. "I used to watch the bailiff coming down, run away and then come back when he'd gone past."

Jack Watkins had been under age when he had enlisted to fight in the Great War. One day he had disappeared and before he could be traced he was in France, serving in the trenches. Fortunate to survive, he returned bearing the scar of a shrapnel wound in his side, a reminder of the harrowing times of which he never cared to speak to his children. Allan remembers him as a gentle even-tempered man: "My father never lifted a hand to any of us.

But mum would. My God she would!" Jack's experiences in the war, Selwyn believes, helped mould his character. "He was very docile, my father, like Allan in a way," he says.

There were few luxuries, but Allan talks fondly of his parents and looks back on a happy childhood in which he had one overriding passion – sport. Despite making sure that he pulled his weight with jobs around the home, his parents always encouraged his interest in cricket. Jack Watkins' first passion may have been for his garden, but he still made time to care for the square at the cricket club. An all-round sportsman, he had been a useful bowler for Usk, and he was still taking wickets for the second eleven when Allan first began playing in the senior team.

The academic side of school life held few attractions for Allan. "All the reports came in and said, 'Albert is not interested in his lessons. All he wants to do is get into the playground and get a ball or bat. He's got a one track mind – and that's sport.' That's what my first master put in my report. My mother gave me a clip at the side of the head about six times because of the reports."

From the local church school Allan moved on to Usk Grammar School. He recalls no searching examination "or I wouldn't have passed in. I learnt less there than I did at the first school. I don't blame the teachers. I just wouldn't work." Even the woodwork class saw Allan finding an outlet for his sporting ambitions. "I got sent home because I went and cut a piece of wood and made a bat. I made this bat and we were playing in the school yard with it and the headmaster came up. 'Where did you get that bat from?' I didn't lie. I said, 'Well, sir...' He said, 'Come with me.' So he took me into the woodwork shed and he took the piece I'd sawn off and he joined it together. He said, 'Funny how the grain meets.' Two of us were involved. We were sent home. Off we went, then after two streets one of the boys came running after us and said, 'The headmaster says you'd better come back.'"

School lessons behind him and his household chores discharged, summer evenings would see Allan rushing up to the cricket ground, not to return until he heard his mother's call from the stile: "Albert, isn't it time you were in bed?" For the youngsters their evenings at the ground usually meant fetching the ball for the senior players in the nets. "Then one day – I'd got a bit bigger, I suppose – they said, 'Come on, young boy, have a bowl.' But for two or three seasons I could only bowl. I couldn't bat or go into the pavilion. Then one day, I couldn't believe it, there were about four of us there and I'd bowled and bowled and one of them said to me 'Albert, go and put your pads on.' I nearly fell through the floor."

Like many young lads consumed with sport, Allan had little time for girls. But Molly Shankland, the sister of one of the youngsters playing at Usk, had taken a shine to Allan with his long floppy hair. "I know it sounds funny but we first saw each other in the fish and chip shop. I was sat with my friends and she went and told her father and mother, 'I've found my boyfriend.' She was only 11 and I didn't know her from Adam."

Almost 70 years after this first encounter they would receive a letter from the Queen congratulating them on their diamond wedding.

Molly had been born in Pontypool and her family had come to live in Usk, and she and Allan went to school together. Molly soon learnt Allan's priorities in life. "She used to play hell when she got older. She used to come and see my mum, 'Where's Albert?' Mum would say, 'Now Molly, where the devil do you think he is?' If I wasn't down at the cricket ground, I was on the football pitch."

Molly with her brother David Shankland

"It was all so innocent in those days," Allan now reflects. "You never dreamt of doing anything wrong from the point of view of boys and girls. Now there are girls of 16 having babies. Is it because they're teaching them all this in school? When we were kids we never even thought about it. Well, I didn't!"

Usk Cricket Club has a proud history, its foundation dating back to 1857 with reports of the game played in the locality from 1770. Back in the 1940s the ground hosted games for Glamorgan Second XI and it continues to do so. Today the club boasts one of the strongest teams in the South Wales League. In the 1930s there was a thriving colts side and in 1933 its captain was Phil Clift. Born in September 1918 and three and a half years older than Allan, Clift was destined to open the batting for Glamorgan and go on to serve

Usk Colts in 1934.
Allan is seated to the right of skipper Phil Clift.

the county as coach and secretary into the 1980s. The young skipper liked the look of the 11-year-old Albert Watkins and ensured that he was picked for the team. "That's where my friendship with Philly started," says Allan, speaking of the man who would become his closest pal in the Glamorgan side and with whom he would still have regular telephone conversations until Clift's death in the early summer of 2005.

There was virtually no cricket played at Usk Grammar School, but Allan looks back on another slice of luck in his quest to learn the game. Managing the Usk colts was a Mr Rickards, an influential member of the club, who lived at Usk Priory, the dominant private house in the centre of the town and one of only four former nunneries in Wales. This imposing home had three driveways, and Allan remembers how Rickards arranged for concrete to be laid over one of them to construct an artificial cricket pitch, on which he welcomed the colts for practice three times a week. Little could Rickards have guessed, as his charges made grateful use of his facilities, that he was helping a boy who would become the first Glamorgan player to hit a Test match century.

At the age of 12 Allan was chosen to play for the Usk first team. Early successes with the bat led to calls to play for Monmouthshire and Glamorgan colts and before long the County Club was taking a serious interest in the young left-hander's progress. By this time Phil Clift was establishing himself with Glamorgan. The first Usk player to be taken onto the county staff, his stylish batting had come to the attention of George Lavis, a member of the county team, who came from nearby Sebastopol and who was later to become a respected county coach. "Philly and George were great friends, like uncle and boy," says Allan, going on to recall how Clift's early promise helped Lavis persuade the county that there was another Usk lad worth having a look at. "He said, 'There's a boy called Albert Watkins; it's worth going to see him.' So Bill Hitch came up, and the next thing I'm on the staff."

A former England fast bowler, Hitch was the Glamorgan coach and he travelled to Usk at the behest of Maurice Turnbull, the county skipper, to put the 15-year-old through his paces. "I must have impressed him," says Allan "because I was invited down to Cardiff to play in a couple of Club and Ground matches." The county officials liked what they saw and for the 1938 season Allan was invited to join the Glamorgan ground staff.

Glamorgan coach Bill Hitch with Phil Clift batting.
Looking on (left) is Willie Jones.

He recalls the financial struggle to manage on thirty shillings a week, as his parents helped scrape together the price of playing kit. "You had to buy all your own stuff, your pads and your trousers. There was nothing given to you." One stroke of luck for Allan was that his friend Phil Clift, whose father was a photographer and owned a small shop in Usk, had been prosperous enough to buy a car. So the pair could share the cost of petrol for the journeys to Cardiff.

Early elation at becoming a professional cricketer soon gave way to frustration and despair as Allan discovered that his successes on village pitches were no guarantee of coping at a higher level. 'I realised very quickly that I had a great deal to learn about the game,' he was to write years later in the *Western Mail*. 'It was one thing to play for Usk and look a winner, but quite a different kettle of fish to hold one's own with experienced professionals. I was beginning to wonder whether I knew anything about the game because it appeared I was doing everything wrong.'

Throughout life Allan has always been plagued by self-doubt. "I lack confidence in everything," he will say even today. So it was when he first found himself mixing with established players at Glamorgan. "If I was in the nets I would stand back and I wouldn't bowl until someone said, 'Come on, Allan, have a bowl.'"

As a young professional Allan was expected to run errands for the senior players and his duties included taking charge of the team's kit when they returned late in the evening from away fixtures. "More than once I missed the last bus from Newport to Usk and had to walk back hoping I could hitch a lift. And I remember Bill Hitch leaving me at Caerleon with eight miles to walk." With George Lavis having departed to take up a professional appointment in Scotland, Allan singles out Arnold Dyson as the senior player whose encouragement kept him going through these difficult early days, but it was still with some misgivings that he returned to cricket in 1939.

Throughout the 1930s there was a meagre budget for a playing staff at Glamorgan and most summers saw a struggle at some stage to find eleven men to take the field. This was the position for the opening championship match of 1939. Wilf Wooller and Johnnie Clay were unavailable and there had been a delay in obtaining the registration of Peter Judge, who was to join from Middlesex as an opening bowler but who was now consigned to the scorer's box. The chosen side was woefully short of bowlers. It read: A.H.Dyson, D.E.Davies, T.L.Brierley, M.J.L.Turnbull, D.Davies, C.C.Smart, E.C.Jones, P.B.Clift, H.D.Davies, A.J.Watkins, J.Mercer. Barely three weeks past his seventeenth birthday, Allan was chosen to make his first-class debut. Although primarily a batsman, he would, remarkably, be opening the bowling with his left-arm medium pacers.

The match was against Nottinghamshire at Trent Bridge, and Allan's great mate Phil Clift would be with him. In later life John Arlott would dub them 'The Two Gentlemen of Usk,' but to the Glamorgan dressing room that day they were Laddie and Nodder. "I was called Nodder," Allan explains, "because I had long hair that used to come down in front of my face. And of course every time I batted I used to be flipping it back."

One who was determined to see his protégés in action was George Lavis. Now playing as a professional with Forfar, he scored a century and took five wickets in Saturday's match for his club before embarking on a seven hour journey to Nottingham to see the second day of Glamorgan's match.

George Lavis

By the time Lavis set off, the makeshift Glamorgan attack had been put to the sword. On a pitch made for batting, the new ball had been entrusted to 44-year-old Jack Mercer, one of the game's great characters. Opposing him was another notorious joker, Charlie Harris. When the second over began Harris had retained the strike. It was a moment for Allan to grab the headlines, at least in his local press, the *South Wales Argus* proclaiming: 'USK BOY OPENS GLAMORGAN'S BOWLING. How Watkins Began His First Big Match.'

Allan started well, but his success was short-lived. 'The youngster's first over to Harris revealed an ability to make the ball swing and was a maiden, but after that he lost his length.' With Harris soon hitting him for three fours, Allan was not alone in struggling to contain the Notts batsmen, who 'could hardly help scoring at 80 an hour.' George Gunn made 119 while Harris, Heane, Hardstaff and Voce all passed fifty, enabling a declaration at the overnight score of 489 for seven. With Glamorgan employing seven different bowlers, Allan was used sparingly, returning figures of 6 - 1 - 38 - 0.

There was little play for George Lavis to watch on the Monday as the Glamorgan openers reached 14 without loss in the only overs the weather permitted. Next day Notts maintained their supremacy on a pitch now freshened by rain and giving the fast bowlers lift and bounce. After the first wicket fell at 34, Bill Voce and Harold Butler made light work of the middle order. At 112 for eight it was Allan's turn to bat. With only six more added he was joined by Jack Mercer. "Jack didn't like batting anyway. He was a number 11 bowler, and he came up to me and said, 'You stay that end and I'll stay this end.' Now it was Bill Voce on at the top end. He bowled me a bouncer, and Joe Hardstaff, a wonderful man, he said, 'What do you think you're bloody well doing? That boy weighs about eight stone, he's 17 years of age and you're bouncing that bloody ball at him.' I can always remember Joe doing that. I was only a youngster and he was a Test player, but we were friends after that."

The Glamorgan innings ended on 130 when Mercer fell to Butler, leaving Allan not out. He had scored 14 of the last 18, the *Western Mail* reporting that he 'showed the right temperament and some of his shots were real gems.' Forced to follow on, Glamorgan fared a little better, playing out time to reach 157 for four, with Allan not required to bat.

From Nottingham the Glamorgan side travelled to Ilford to play Essex. In a match whose shape was dictated by the weather, Allan played no part with bat or ball as declarations enabled Glamorgan to win by five wickets. The team moved on to Hove and a Glamorgan defeat by an innings and 79 runs. For Allan there were 11 unproductive overs in Sussex's innings, sandwiched between two failures with the bat as he was bowled in both innings by Jack Nye for scores of 3 and 4. Seeing one of his bails flying a measured 33 yards served to remind the young Watkins that he was now playing a man's game.

With Peter Judge's registration formalised and Austin Matthews also able to play from late July, there was little further need of Allan's services, though he took part in a heavy defeat against Warwickshire at Edgbaston and on 2 August he was chosen to make his home début against Yorkshire at the Arms Park in

Cardiff. He spent hours practising in the nets with Bill Hitch in the days before the match. A natural hooker, he had been learning to restrain the shot and play straight. It was a painful lesson as Hitch's deliveries rose and rapped him in the ribs.

Match day came and Allan stripped off in the dressing room. "It was Arnold Dyson, he looked and said to me, 'Oh my God, Allan, what the hell has happened to you?' I was black and blue all over the ribs. So of course Maurice Turnbull saw me. 'Turn round,' he said, 'who the hell has done that?' And of course I didn't want to tell him. 'Put your shirt on,' he said, 'you can't play like that.' So I didn't play against Yorkshire. Bill Hitch was in trouble after that, and I always thought that Bill thought it was me that told Turnbull, but I didn't. I didn't say a word. I just took my clothes off."

The Glamorgan team in 1939.
Standing (l to r): Phil Clift, Cyril Smart, Haydn Davies, Peter Judge, Closs Jones,
Tom Brierley, Allan Watkins.
Seated (l to r): Arnold Dyson, Dai Davies, Maurice Turnbull, Jack Mercer,
Emrys Davies.

Allan still remembers this match for giving him the chance to meet Maurice Leyland, his particular hero and the player on whom Bill Hitch had advised him to model his own game. Allan had watched the left-handed Leyland make 127 at Cardiff the year before and he now found his idol happy to pass on advice. "Maurice was like me, short legs, short arms and all that. And he told me three things. A left-hander with short legs, you don't drive through the covers unless the ball is right underneath you. Anything on the middle and leg or leg stick, you sweep it. The other thing he did was change my grip so I could stretch another foot and a half forward. That's all I learnt and I stuck to that throughout my life."

When Allan's home début finally came, the second innings of a drawn match against Northants brought him the first of his 833 first-class wickets, when he bowled Jack Timms. In the same match he hit an undefeated 23, his highest score of a modest first season, which brought 57 runs at an average of 19 and a single wicket at a cost of 187. There were a couple of Second Eleven friendlies, with useful knocks for Allan, but serious cricket was over for six long years. Had it not been so, a permanent spot in the Glamorgan side might not have been long in coming. Bill Hitch spoke of his progress to the local press: "I have seldom had a youngster more eager to learn. Watkins will do everything he is told, and he is quick to remedy little faults. That is one of the reasons why he should get on. His display against Notts was particularly encouraging."

Allan himself was so young. He had no idea what war might mean for the shape of his life. "I was too young to be called up even, just seventeen and a half," he recalls. "Of course, I hoped I'd be able to play again eventually, but none of us knew what was going to happen."

Chapter Two
An Easy War For Stoker Watkins

Though Allan could not have known it, the declaration of war meant that he had played for the last time under the captaincy of the aristocratic Maurice Turnbull. For the labourer's son from Usk, the skipper-cum-secretary was a daunting figure. "He was a bit of an upper crust, not only with me but all the players." This had been Phil Clift's view too: "We had to stand to attention in his office." But Allan also recalls Turnbull's indomitable spirit on the field, where his talent shone through to the last, with 156 in Glamorgan's final match, against Leicestershire at Aylestone Road.

Off the field, too, there was style and panache in all that Turnbull did. "He was a madman, in a car at least. He didn't think that red lights in Cardiff mattered. Evidently he got killed in the war doing the same thing. The orders were to retreat, but he got fed up of retreating so he thought, 'To hell with this, I'm going to advance.' And he got himself mown down. That would be typical of Maurice Turnbull." A major in the Welsh Guards, Turnbull lost his life bravely, on 5 August, 1944, mown down by machine gun fire as he tried to immobilise the leading vehicle in a column of German tanks making their way down a narrow lane near Montchamp in Normandy.

Turnbull had been the inspiration behind Glamorgan's fight for financial survival throughout the 1930s, and one of his last duties was to write to the players at the end of the 1939 season. "I've still got his letter," Allan said, rummaging in his desk. Dated 21 September, it informed him of the closing down of the office and the termination of his contract. The letter continued:

> 'Realising the hardship involved for you, the Committee has voted you one month's winter salary to be paid immediately and cheque is enclosed. In addition £100 talent money has been awarded and will be distributed next week together with any balances due to you.'

"I never got that £100," Allan says without rancour. At least he had received his basic salary: "Thirty shillings a week!"

Still awaiting call-up, Allan was able to enjoy some cricket for Usk during the summer of 1940, a highlight of his season coming in the match against Ross, when he hit 38 off an eight-ball over. When his papers finally arrived, Allan chose to join the Royal Navy. Basic training took him to Malvern and after four or five weeks, to his surprise, he was retained as an assistant instructor. "Why they should pick on me of all the people in my group, I don't know. I helped the PO on the square bashing and all that."

Missing a gunnery course on which he should have been sent, Stoker Watkins was posted to Devonport. "There were about 60 of us and the CO came and said, 'Right, that half that way, and that half that way.' The half I was in went down to Granby Barracks, and that's where I stayed for the whole of the war." The arbitrary split of the group meant that Allan was dealt a lucky hand. He admits to having had an easy war, consigned to fire-fighting duties around Devonport. Though Plymouth was mercilessly attacked by German bombers, the civilian fire brigade had responsibility for the safety of the city. Allan, meanwhile, was among those charged with looking after the docks, where he reckons only about three bombs fell. So he had time on his hands and plenty of opportunity for sport.

Running sport in the forces, Allan soon discovered, was a much sought after job. "A lot of people used to come into the forces, 'Oh, I played for Aston Villa, I played for Chelsea.' They were all looking for one of these jobs." The sport at the barracks, when Allan arrived, was looked after by a former headmaster, now a Petty Officer, assisted by a senior stoker, Ivor Givlin, a talented footballer from Swansea. "Between them these two ran the sport. I went down and they said, 'What was your job?' I said, 'Cricketer.' The PO said, 'That's a funny thing to put down as a job.' So he sent for Givlin. 'Never heard of the bloody fellow!'"

Arriving in the winter, with his name ringing no bells, Allan had been regarded as a sporting nonentity, but once spring arrived and the talk turned to cricket, he put his name down to play. The hopefuls assembled at the nets and Allan started bowling spinners on the concrete pitch until it was Givlin's turn to bat. "I thought I'll teach him a bloody lesson. So I bounced it. It went about two feet above his head. The PO was stood there, 'What the hell's going on?'

So I said, 'I'm having a bowl. I'm a fast bowler.' 'Oh, that's better. I can understand that.' From that ball on we were great friends."

Once he saw Allan bat, it was clear to Givlin that he had a player of exceptional talent on his hands, and Givlin's wife in Swansea was able to write reassuring him that Allan was indeed known to be a county cricketer. There were several other useful players at Devonport, and the pitch at nearby Mount Wise, on which the matches were played, was a beauty. "As good as any first-class wicket in England," Allan claims. Opportunities to play came thick and fast. "The word got about that we were a good cricket side, so of course everybody challenged us, including the Australian Army, who were down there with their flying boats." One year Stoker Watkins hit 930 runs and took 125 wickets for the barracks, receiving, silver-mounted, the ball with which he had taken his hundredth wicket. "We had some wonderful games," he recalls. "I was lent out now and again to the Officers' Mess side. And I think I was the only stoker to play for the Navy at Lord's."

It was the same story with football. Before joining the Navy, Allan's game had been rugby. Though he had always kicked a soccer ball around as a youngster, it was at rugby, with the Usk Club, that he had first played in adult company, as a scrum half. Short and

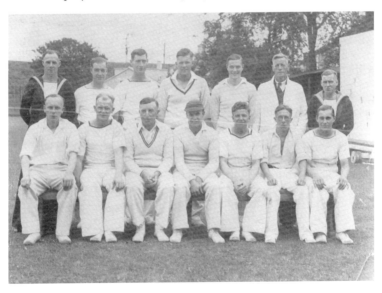

Allan, seated centre, with The Granby Barracks cricket team
who were runners-up in the Devonport RN & RM League Championship in 1943.

stocky, he was the ideal build for the position and such was his talent that, during the first winter of the war, when he had been too young to enlist, Allan had attracted the attention of Pontypool, one of the major clubs in South Wales. There he played in a match against the wartime All Blacks, and he enjoyed a brief association with Bleddyn Williams, later to become a legend of Welsh rugby.

Allan recalls an early match report that had sung the praises of the young Williams: "Although it said the Pontypool pack was well beaten, it praised Bleddyn Williams for scoring three times. What I want to know is if we were behind a beaten pack and I was the scrum half, how the hell did I get the ball out to Bleddyn Williams to score three times without getting a mention?"

At Granby Barracks, Allan found that there were no opportunities for rugby, so he began to play soccer more seriously. His natural talent for any sport – he could turn his hand to badminton, table tennis, boxing or shooting – meant that he quickly adapted to the round ball code, and he was a prominent member of a Granby Barracks team powerful enough to take on all comers. A notable highlight came when the barracks side beat Plymouth Argyle, a Second Division League side, in the final of the South West Cup. Allan, left-handed in all he did on the cricket field, favoured his left foot on the football pitch and played at left half. He remembers it as one of the hardest-working positions on the field. "That heavy ball I can remember. Being a wing-half you took your head to all the goal kicks. The opposition kicking the ball always landed it in the wing half's position."

Plymouth Argyle's scouts had already been casting an eye over the talent in the naval sides. They had spotted Tommy Briggs, who would go on to play for England B as a centre forward and set a scoring record with seven goals in a match for Blackburn Rovers against Bristol Rovers, and the victory of the Granby Barracks team emphasised the quality of some of the other players. Allan was one to whom the club made approaches and, as soon as he was demobbed in 1945, he signed professional terms.

By this time Allan was a married man and a father. When war came, Molly had been able to join up before Allan. She had volunteered for the WAAF, and Allan remembers her returning to Usk. He was in Twyn Square, the main gathering place for youngsters in the town, when Molly arrived with a group of girls. One of them came up to him. "'Molly wants to talk to you.' I said, 'Well I don't want to talk to her.' 'Oh yes you do,' she said. I said 'Why should I?' And all this nonsense. She said, 'Come on Albert, go and talk to her.' So that was it – I never knew anybody else!"

By the time Allan was at Devonport, Molly had been posted to Weston-super-Mare. Nearly three years into the war, the mood was one of great uncertainty. "We didn't know at that time whether one of us might be killed, so we decided to get married." It came as a shock to his mother when Allan announced his engagement, but

the pair duly celebrated their wedding at St Mary's, the Norman church in the centre of Usk, where both had been communicants. Allan remembers a naval friend, Rodney York, greeting them as they came down the path from the church. "Well, Watkins," he said, "that's one bloody knot you won't be able to undo!"

St Mary's, Usk,
where Allan and Molly were married

There was a brief honeymoon in London, where two of Allan's sisters were now living. It was while they were in the capital that a photograph of the couple, both in uniform, was taken. For many years the little snap shot with a partially failed exposure was the only memento of their wedding that Allan and Molly possessed. To celebrate their parents' diamond anniversary, the couple's children arranged for the picture to be enlarged and

The only photograph of the newly weds

printed onto a white canvas. It now hangs beside the fireplace in Allan's Oundle home.

Allan had been contemplating a possible transfer, still as a fire fighter, to Australia. He soon found that, not surprisingly, such a move would not have been popular with those running the sport at Devonport, and he was dissuaded. Then, to his surprise, he learnt from a superior officer that it would be possible for his new wife to join him at Plymouth. "Don't you know that the Navy can claim a wife?" he said. "I'll ring the authorities and get your wife transferred down here." So Allan and Molly found themselves in digs, well cared for by an elderly landlady, of whom they grew very fond. But Molly's days in the forces were soon to come to an end when she announced that she was pregnant. She returned to Usk for the birth of young Allen, the first of the couple's four children, in April 1944.

When Allan returned to Plymouth for the season of 1946/47, he went ahead of Molly. The couple now had a second son, David, and Allan was looking for a home where he could house his family. He was fortunate to meet a dockyard worker, Ed Stere, a middle-aged bachelor who owned a bungalow overlooking the sea at nearby Whitsands. "As soon as he heard that I'd signed up for Plymouth Argyle, he said to me, 'Would you and Molly like to join me in my bungalow?'"

Molly travelled to Plymouth to see the property. To reach the bungalow meant taking a ferry across the Tamar. The journey continued by bus and ended with a mile and a half on foot. It was worth the effort. The moment Molly saw the bungalow on the cliff top with its breath-taking views across the bay, she fell in love with the spot.

Allan found the arrangement with Ed Stere embarrassingly generous. "I didn't pay any rent. We used to have terrible rows. I used to say to him, 'This is ridiculous.' But he used to come and watch the football matches. He was mad on Plymouth Argyle and he thought he was doing it for Plymouth Argyle, not for me!"

For Molly it was bliss to live beside the sea. In summers to come she would return to Whitsands with the family and stay with 'Uncle Ed'. The young children became known as 'the Water Babes' as they ran free on the beach and splashed around in the rock pools. There were days of endless sunshine, but Allen also cherishes memories of childhood evenings when the weather changed and they had to put up the shutters against the buffeting of the onshore gales as they gathered beside oil-filled lamps in a bungalow that had never known gas or electricity.

Throughout her life Molly would look back on time spent at Whitsands as the happiest days of her life, choosing the bay as the place where her ashes should be scattered.

Chapter Three
A Foothold in County Cricket

Despite his success in matches played with the Navy, Allan knew he had achieved little as a county cricketer and, when the first post-war football season ended, he looked for a more secure future for his young family. Returning from Plymouth, he resumed a career as a baker, which he had briefly begun on leaving school. News that their own Albert Watkins was turning his back on first-class cricket to make doughnuts and fancy cakes spread round Usk and reached the ears of Mr A.D.Pollock, the headmaster who had despaired of Allan finding a career other than in sport. Now he wrote to his former pupil, reminding him of the sacrifices his parents had made to help with the cost of kit and paying fares for him to reach his matches. "He told me to get back to cricket. He said I could make the grade if I tried."

With Molly's encouragement, Allan decided to give professional cricket another go, and on 14 June, 1946 he was back in the county team for their match against Essex at Chelmsford. The captain now was Johnnie Clay, whose long career stretched back to Glamorgan's first championship season in 1921. In earlier years he had used his height as a fast-medium bowler, but it was after converting to off spin that he became one of the most successful bowlers in the land, winning a Test cap in 1935. As with so many other counties, he had faced many hurdles with Glamorgan to get the show back on the road in this first post-war season. "I don't know what we're going to do," he is quoted as saying. "We lost everything during the war. We have no records, but we'll get a few lads together, and at least we'll turn up for every match."

Johnnie Clay

As an uncapped player, Allan returned to a wage of no more than four pounds a week. "I used to go to Usk and look at the roadmen sweeping the roads, and in the back of my mind I used to think to myself, 'Well why have I got all this worry about cricket and form when I could be doing that for more or less the same money?'"

Despite their slender resources Glamorgan had begun their season well with three wins and two losses in the seven matches before Allan joined the team, and by the end of the summer, at the age of 48, Clay would have taken 130 wickets at 13.40 and led his side to sixth place in the Championship. Like his good friend Turnbull before him, the Winchester-educated Clay, with his racehorses and a fine home at Cowbridge, came from a different world from Allan.

Though holding a regular place in the side, Allan, usually batting at seven, found runs elusive in a wet summer that often saw the bowlers take command, but 14 in his first innings of the season was the top score in a Glamorgan total of 50 against Essex. 'The way he set his teeth and stuck there at a very awkward time was an object lesson,' wrote former Glamorgan cricketer E.R.K.Glover in the *Western Mail.* There were 100 minutes of defiance in a top-scoring 44 not out against Middlesex at Swansea, but this was followed by three ducks in a row, and after 15 completed innings Allan had garnered just 167 runs. Moreover, the young man who had started his county career by taking the new ball was asked to bowl only eight overs all summer.

Only Allan's fielding was contributing much to the side's success. This was the year in which he first took his place in the leg trap, holding 18 catches in his 16 matches. Allan had begun his career as an out-fielder, and he was not one of the best: "I wasn't too quick in the outfield, being a small chap. And I dropped a few catches. Then one day we were playing at Pontypridd. Austin Matthews was bowling and a few balls went down the leg side as catches, and he said, 'I'd like to have a fielder there.' So I was called in to short leg, and I caught one or two. So I was told, 'That's your position now.'" It was Arnold Dyson who was always ready with a useful tip for the new close catcher. "I remember taking a catch one day and I'd gone a long way left. I was on the floor with the ball in my left hand and Arnold was at forward short leg. And all he said was: 'How many times have I got to tell thee? Don't anticipate.'"

Noting that Allan had held many fine catches, a local paper reported that 'none was better than that which dismissed Wally Hammond at Cardiff in the recent Gloucestershire match.' Allan remembers it well. "Johnnie Clay had said, 'Anyone who gets this fellow out for under ten, there's a tenner for you.' Well, as it happened, I caught Wally for eight at leg slip. I never saw my tenner though. I thought, 'You mean bugger!'"

Despite this incident, Clay was a man Allan regarded with affection and respect: "A very nice chap. Without him there wouldn't have been a Glamorgan. He was the person who really kept Glamorgan going when they were desperate for money, him and a fellow called HH Merrett, who became president of the club. And what a terrific bowler! I reckon he was the finest off-spinner I've seen. He was so tall that he didn't have to loop the ball; it looped itself."

Allan had still to make much impact on the first-class game when the time came for him to return to Plymouth for the winter. As he bade farewell to his team-mates, he feared that he might be on the verge of an early exit from county cricket. However, even for a couple of matches, Glamorgan had no ready replacement. "Do you think you could play one more match for us tomorrow?" Johnnie Clay asked. There was a telephone call to Plymouth Argyle. Allan was given permission to extend his cricket season and took his place in the side to meet Surrey at Cardiff.

Glamorgan won the toss and decided to bat in glorious weather before a crowd of nearly 10,000. They started badly and were still in trouble when Allan joined Arthur Porter at 82 for five. Dominating a partnership of 132, he was 109 not out at stumps, 'playing shots of rare promise towards the close of the day'. "I was a bit nervous when I went in," Allan says. "Because I thought 'What are Glamorgan going to do with me?' Then, when I got the hundred, it was wonderful." He remained undefeated next day with 119, when the innings closed on 305, to share with Emrys Davies the season's highest score by a Glamorgan batsman.

With Surrey twice bowled out cheaply and Glamorgan needing just two runs for victory, Allan made the winning hit. Meanwhile, letters and telegrams arrived to mark his splendid knock, among them one from Bill Hitch, who had always believed the boy from Usk would make it. 'Keep your chin up and take your success calmly and you should have a good future,' wrote former captain Trevor Arnott. A shorter pencilled note came from the hand that had so often wielded the cane at Usk Grammar School. 'Well done, Albert!' wrote A.D.Pollock. 'I am delighted to have seen your first century in first-class cricket. May you build a mighty successful career on today's great innings.'

There was one more match, against Nottinghamshire at Ebbw Vale, which brought Allan 35 runs, enabling him to boost his average to 20.37, sixth in the county list, before football finally claimed him for the winter. Had he left a week earlier, he would have been walking away into an uncertain world, but now he knew there would be a job awaiting him when he returned to Glamorgan in the spring.

As Allan looks back on his time in professional football, he makes clear that it brought him none of the pleasure and camaraderie of his years in first-class cricket. "No comparison," he says emphatically. "Cricketers, you live with them and you might have had your arguments with them; but that would only be an argument. With soccer players it was nasty." Most of Allan's time at Plymouth was spent in the reserves, and he still vents his frustration that, notwithstanding the threat of relegation, the first team was a closed shop. "The bloody players were picking the side, not the manager," he says. Allan had a supporter in Arthur Gorman, who was in charge of the reserves. "He went and said,

Allan scores against Swansea Town, his only goal for Plymouth Argyle.

'What the hell have I got Watkins in the side for? He should be in the first side – he's streets ahead of anybody else.'"

Once given a place in the first team, Allan found little help from those who were supposed to be his team-mates. "I didn't like the atmosphere. I didn't like the attitude of the players. It's amazing in the old days how they could play you off the field. You're running alongside somebody who's got the ball and you shout for it. He'll look and he'll give you the ball seconds after you've shouted for it – and you collect the opposition at the same time. The only help I got was from the full back, who eventually went up to Notts County as manager. I know it's an awful thing to say but there were three or four lads towards the end of the season going for treatment and there was nothing wrong with them. They just didn't want to play."

The winter of 1946/47 is remembered as one of the severest of the century. Snow lay over Britain for weeks on end, taking its toll of all outdoor sport, and the football season had to be extended to complete the fixtures. Allan faced a clash of loyalties as cricket was getting under way. "The Plymouth chairman said, 'The season's extended.' I said, 'Not bloody likely. I'm going to Wales, I'm playing my cricket.' He said, 'You can't do that – you're under contract.' I said, 'Waste of bloody paper because I'm going.' And, of course, I did break my contract. I went."

Wilf Wooller

Back at Glamorgan, where Wilf Wooller was now captain, Allan began the new season slowly. There were fifties against Yorkshire and Surrey, but a run of modest scores ended with a vengeance against Northants in early July. His 146 in that match was the first of four championship centuries. The second came two matches later, against Worcestershire at Ebbw Vale. One who saw the whole of this match was John Arlott. Apart from the five Tests against South Africa, his book of the season, *Gone to the Cricket*, covered just two other games, the tourists' traditional opener at Worcester and Glamorgan's championship match with Worcestershire at Ebbw Vale.

In his early days of cricket commentating, Arlott still had much to learn about the intricacies of the game. To redress this problem, he befriended the players, finding his way into county dressing rooms in a way that no reporter had previously attempted. He found a welcome at Glamorgan, where a strangely enduring friendship built up between the liberal broadcaster and the notoriously right wing Wilfred Wooller, who offered Arlott regular hospitality whenever he came to Wales. "Although he always gave the illusion that he was up to his ears in first-class cricket, he wasn't really," Wooller told Arlott's biographer, David Rayvern Allen. Winning the trust of Wooller and others in the Glamorgan team meant that Arlott always retained a soft spot for the cricketers from the Principality, whose cause he was quick to espouse. As Haydn Davies once confided with a rascally smile, "We used to tell him what to put in his reports."

Winning the toss at Ebbw Vale, Wooller decided to bat on a dampish pitch. The captain made 42 in half an hour, but the match was tilting Worcestershire's way when Allan went in at 62 for three. By close of play he was unbeaten on 88, and Arlott wrote of what he had seen:

> 'Watkins of Usk is probably the most interesting young left-hand bat now in English first-class cricket. Short, grey-faced and quiet, he has immense possibilities. His play is built upon an almost impregnable defence: primarily and basically his wicket is safe. His run-scoring strokes are built on to, not tacked upon, his defence. He balances those strokes, playing on either side of the wicket. Hence he has no 'characteristic' shot in the sense of a stroke which he might be tempted to employ against the ball not absolutely suitable for it. Two more seasons of county cricket should see him so versed in the tricks of the trade – for he is a shrewd and perceptive man, with his heart and brain in cricket – that his selection for England is automatic. He will make many runs against the best bowling because he has a calm cricketing temperament, a cricketing brain, and a technique of batsmanship which is sound to the last detail. He is also a brilliant short leg, frequently catching the uncatchable.'

Monday's play saw Allan complete his century and reach 111 before 'speeding up, he was beaten by Jenkins' leg break and Yarnold stumped him with immense gusto.'

Allan had now made number five his regular place in the order, as it would be for many years to come. After the game at Ebbw Vale, a steady stream of useful scores followed, culminating in a match against Somerset made memorable for Allan by the antics of Wilf Wooller. "The whole thing about Wilf was that he liked to skipper both sides. I remember we played at Weston-super-Mare and their second innings went on and on and he wanted them to declare. 'This is ridiculous,' he was saying and he got more and more irate because they didn't declare to give us a chance. Eventually they did declare. So we got into the dressing room and he said, 'Right, you know what to do. Put the bloody door up if that's the way they want to play cricket.' We got a good start. I was number four and I joined George Lavis – he was a good batsman but he had no temperament – but he was doing well this time. He said, 'Come on, we can win this match.' So George and I went for it. We got the score up and eventually won the match. When we got in, the skipper never said a word. You could see he had a grin on his face. Some of the committee came in – because it was the Weston match and they always used to come over on the boat – and they said, 'Well done, Wilf!' And Wilf said, 'Yes, when I tell them to do one thing and they do another!'"

Allan made 105 that day. He was out shortly before victory came with two minutes to spare. Two matches later there was another century, 110 in the defeat of Surrey at the Arms Park.

Allan receiving a clock at the Usk CC dinner to mark his fine season in 1947

That winter, when the Usk Cricket Club held their dinner at The Three Salmons Hotel, Allan's family were there to see the club celebrate his fine season with the presentation of an inscribed clock. His county skipper addressed the diners, passing on the verdict of the South African tourists' manager that he had never seen a better close fielder on the leg side than Allan and adding prophetically, 'I have no doubt that one day he will play for England.' With 1,407 runs at an average of 33.50 and 27 catches Allan had become a key member of the Glamorgan side, and the award of his county cap set the seal on a fine season. But Allan was not yet the all-rounder he was to become. Throughout the summer he had bowled not a single over, despite playing in a side in which most players turned an arm in an attack which, though strengthened by the arrival of Len Muncer, was now deprived of Austin Matthews, Peter Judge and, except for a few matches, Johnnie Clay.

As the cricket season closed, Allan determined that he was not returning to Plymouth, where he had become so disenchanted with the weakness of the Argyle manager and where, despite the generosity of Ed Stere, the cost of running a second home had left him out of pocket. He had hoped that he might take up rugby once more but, to his intense disappointment, he soon found that this was impossible: "As a professional cricketer I could play amateur rugby, but as a professional soccer player I couldn't. So I couldn't play any rugby." So rigid was the bar to any participation that Allan's brother Selwyn, also an all-round sportsman, recalls being rejected when he went over to the rugby ground to give the Usk juniors some help with their place kicking. "I went over there, telling them to use the in-step rather than the toe, and all of a sudden I was told, 'You can't do this – you're a professional.'"

Rejected by rugby, Allan took a winter at leisure before deciding, shortly before the end of the season, to give soccer another go. He and Molly were still living in Usk, where they had rooms first above the Bridge Inn across the river from the town centre, later taking a flat above a bank overlooking Twyn Square. This time Allan vowed to make sure that he would find a club closer to home. He recalls the chance to join Cardiff City, like Argyle in the then Second Division, whose chairman happened to be H.H. (soon to be Sir Herbert) Merrett, whom he knew as president of Glamorgan. Merrett was also chairman of Powell Duffryn, to whose offices Allan was summoned. "I went down to Tiger Bay, as it was called then, to his office. Well what an office! The staff at the door said, 'Do you know H.H.?' I said, 'Well I've talked to him.' They said 'You must know him well – he doesn't ask many people into his office.' And I'm not surprised. It was about twenty times as big as this room, and the carpet was that blooming thick."

Cardiff City was one of the stronger clubs in the Second Division when Allan signed. His plan was to play for his new club in the winter of 1948/49. At that time he could not have guessed that England's cricket selectors would have other plans for him.

Chapter Four
Called Up For England

Sixth in 1946 and ninth the next year, the Glamorgan players had no reason for lofty aspirations as they assembled for the start of the 1948 season. This was to be remembered as the summer in which Don Bradman's all-conquering Australians would hold centre stage, but from its earliest weeks it was also the year in which Wilfred Wooller's Glamorgan would set the pace in the County Championship.

With seven victories and just one loss in their first nine championship matches, Glamorgan emerged as the early leaders, but for Allan the runs were flowing less freely than in the hot summer of 1947. An early century at Worcester was followed by nine innings before he next passed fifty. But there was now

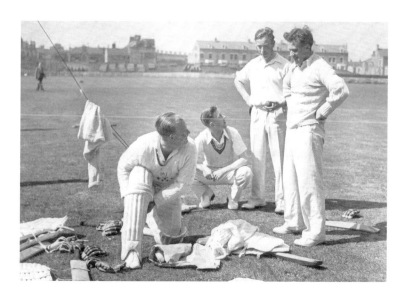

Pre-season nets, 1948.
Allan with (l to r) Jim Eaglestone, Norman Hever and Phil Clift

another string to his bow: from the first match he was regarded as a regular member of the attack.

Allan recalls the part that Arnold Dyson played in his re-establishment as a bowler. At the pre-season nets, before moving north to take up a new appointment as coach at Oundle School, Dyson had observed Allan bowling spinners. "He said, 'You didn't bowl like that before the war. Why are you doing it now?' I said, 'Because that's what everybody said I had to do.' He said, 'Don't be so bloody stupid. Where's the ball? Now bowl!' He made Wilf come over and he said, 'Have you seen this boy?' Because he still called me 'boy' though I was a man and married. 'Right, Allan,' he said, 'now bowl.' So Wilf looked. 'Bloody hell!' he said, and before long I was bowling."

The 1948 season opened in traditional fashion at Worcester, where the Australians met the county in the first match of their tour. No other first-class cricket was scheduled on that late April day and in the crowd was Allan Watkins, sent up from Usk by Wilfred Wooller. "He told me to go and watch Ernie Toshack." Toshack was the unsung workhorse of the Australian attack, mixing his left-arm swingers and cutters and varying his pace while maintaining an unrelenting leg-stump line. His role was to keep things tight while Lindwall and Miller recharged their batteries. Wooller saw Allan as a bowler capable of bringing this same control and variety to the Glamorgan attack. Soon labelling him 'Tosh', his team-mates did not let Allan forget whose bowling he was striving to emulate.

Allan looks back to the times they had with Wooller as captain, the arguments and the tensions, but he is quick to pay tribute to his skipper's shrewd cricketing brain and the help he offered. "He made me as a bowler. I wouldn't have been anything like the bowler I became, if it hadn't been for Wilf Wooller. He always set the field, though there'd be variation if the bowler thought there should be variation – he'd stop and listen. I bowled in-duckers and I had three short legs, a fine leg and two more back on the leg side, one slip, cover point and mid off. If the ball was swinging more, the one from square would go back to make two behind, but he was mostly square. And if I strayed and bowled one down the off side Wilf would be at forward short leg and he'd give me a look. 'What do you think you're bloody well doing? Why have I set your field over here when you're bowling over there?' If he did it once he did it a dozen times."

The early spells were steady, but the first five matches with his revived quicker style of bowling brought Allan only two wickets. Four cheap scalps at Derby, in Glamorgan's only early season defeat, suggested better times ahead, but there were few remarkable spells and, when Glamorgan began their match with Warwickshire at Neath on 24 July, he had only 24 victims. In the weeks leading into this match the Welshmen had gone off the boil. Draws at Northampton and Hull were followed by a crushing 183-run defeat by Warwickshire at Edgbaston and another much narrower loss to Leicestershire at Cardiff. From these four matches Glamorgan had taken not a single point. Their early season bounce was becoming a distant memory, and they had seen Derbyshire succeed them at the top of the table.

Their visit to Neath did not bring an immediate change to the Welsh county's fortunes. For the sixth match in a row Wilf Wooller lost the toss, and his team were compelled to take the field. On an easy-paced pitch 'play proceeded sedately for nearly an hour and then things began to happen.' Allan came on at 27 for no wicket. Immediately he bowled Gardner. In his next over the New Zealander Donnelly fell, also bowled. After a brief Warwickshire recovery, Ord was bowled as soon as Allan returned to the attack and, when he also hit the stumps of Spooner and Grove, he had taken five wickets, all bowled, to record his best analysis to date: 16 – 6 – 19 – 5.

All out for 122, Warwickshire faced steady batting from a rejuvenated Glamorgan side, who built a lead of 132 on first innings. There was no repeat of Allan's magic when Warwickshire batted a second time, finally setting a fourth innings target of 104. This proved to be 'a task they found none too easy on a wearing pitch against the guile of Hollies' but, thanks to a resolute knock from Willie Jones, victory was secured by three wickets. Now Glamorgan were back on track in pursuit of the title.

Eight thousand had packed into the Gnoll at Neath and, when Glamorgan moved along the coast to the St Helen's ground at Swansea, more than 50,000 paid to see the Australians, a game that, for local supporters, had the flavour of their own 'Test match'. Allan made 19 before falling to Lindwall, and he later won an lbw decision against opener Sidney Barnes before torrential rain ended the match on the second afternoon. Allan's innings had contained two thunderous hooks to the boundary off Miller, but it was his friend Phil Clift whose cameo 30 took the eye of the

Australian captain, Don Bradman later naming him as one of the most promising young players he had seen on the trip.

Rain was now threatening to shape the destiny of the Championship, but Glamorgan managed one crucial victory: between damp draws with Gloucestershire and Middlesex, they bowled out Somerset at Weston for 96 to win by eight runs. Four for 27 in the Gloucestershire match at Ebbw Vale brought Allan's tally of wickets to 35 at 28.23 each. With the bat he was still failing to re-capture his best form of 1947, averaging 26.71, with only three fifties to accompany his early season century. His value to any team was crucially boosted by a growing reputation as one of the most prehensile close fielders in the land, but with bat and ball he was still making his way to journeyman status on the county circuit. So when the selectors met to pick their team for the fifth Test at The Oval, with England already trailing by three matches to none, most followers would have agreed with the cricket correspondent of *The Times*, when he wrote that 'the choice of Watkins may cause some surprise.'

"I nearly fell through the floor when I heard. It was Wilf who told me. Then we heard it over the wireless – there was no television – and Molly couldn't believe it. I knew, but I didn't say much about it. I said, 'I think I might be playing.'" Adding to the public incredulity, and to Allan's own astonishment, was the news that he would open the bowling. "Why I came to be an opening bowler, I haven't a clue. I wasn't an opening bowler for Glamorgan."

Allan's selection, at the age of 26, answered the call for youth and, if Glamorgan's domestic success was to be rewarded, there were few other candidates for the honour of a Test cap – Len Muncer perhaps, the first bowler to take a hundred wickets in the season, or Willie Jones, who had enjoyed a purple patch with two double hundreds in June, or skipper Wooller, who had to turn down the vice-captaincy of MCC that winter, but the Welsh county was proud to call itself a side of few stars. Allan believes that his good friend John Arlott, keen to see the selectors looking further afield, had helped to press his cause, but perhaps more pertinent was the presence on the selection panel of the Glamorgan secretary and Allan's former skipper, John Clay.

It was a red letter day for South Wales. 'They will be toasting Allan Watkins, the Glamorgan left-hander, in the picturesque, oak-beamed inns and taverns in and around rural Usk tonight,' wrote the *South Wales Argus*, later suggesting that for cricket lovers it had brought the market town 'a distinction it has not known since the Marcher Lords made it an important meeting place back in the fourteenth century!'

Allan was rested from the Middlesex match ahead of the Test, which began on Saturday 14 August, but such concessions were not the normal practice in those days. Even with a Saturday start, the rest of the team were all engaged in county matches that had begun on the Wednesday. Rain spared Norman Yardley and Len Hutton from taking the field on the last day at Scarborough, but for Allan's new ball partner, Alec Bedser, it had been business as usual leading the attack for Surrey at Weston. The day before the Test match was due to begin, Bedser spent most of his time in the field, delivering no fewer than 59 overs over the three days of the match against Somerset. "He was fantastic, Alec," says Allan. "You talk about these modern bowlers. You could put Alec on one end and forget he was there."

There was no team hotel at which to assemble, no chance for a get-together on the eve of the match as the players made their way to London from around the country. Allan chose to stay with his oldest sister Millie, who lived at Hither Green in South-East London. On the day of the match he made his way to The Oval, as he would for a Glamorgan game, arriving for his first Test by bus. His bag in hand, he made his way through the gate and up to the dressing room to meet the rest of the team.

As the Olympic Games captured the nation's interest in the north of the capital, a saturated outfield delayed play at The Oval before Norman Yardley, on winning a toss he might have been happy to lose, decided that England should bat. With Cyril Washbrook nursing an injured thumb, Len Hutton set out for a sawdust-covered square partnered by John Dewes, a Cambridge Blue and, like Allan, a left-hander making his debut. Dewes soon looked out of his depth, and when he played across the line to be bowled by Miller, his dismissal set in motion the most ignominious batting collapse in England's Test history. As Hutton alone stood firm, Edrich, Compton, Crapp and Yardley all fell to the Australian pace attack. Shortly after lunch, at 35 for five, Allan went in to join Hutton.

'This was the first game of any calibre Watkins had played away from his Glamorgan county, so he must have felt very strange about everything,' wrote Jack Fingleton. "I didn't know any of the team really," Allan agrees. "I felt a bit lonely. And coming from a side of Welshmen, you know how noisy they can be. With Glamorgan there was a lot of back chat and pulling your leg, and suddenly I was in a team that were all individuals. It was sort of quiet and a bit dignified really." Allan found a soul mate in Eric Hollies, and several others would become good friends in South Africa, but in his first Test Allan felt that he hardly belonged in the England dressing room.

It was no more welcoming in the middle as he faced up to the world's most feared fast bowler with three wickets already under his belt. "Lindwall bounced me," he recalls, "and of course I was always a hooker. He hit me on the shoulder and it went down to third man somewhere." Soon Allan was struck on the pads, playing across a ball from Bill Johnston. "Dai Davies said he had great pleasure giving me out lbw!" 42 for 6, when Allan was dismissed, would soon become 52 all out. Only once, in Test cricket's earliest days, had an England team been dismissed for fewer.

Still awaiting his first Test run, Allan retired to the dressing room where he found Herbert Strudwick. "I pulled off my clothes and Struddy said, 'Christ, Allan, what the hell's happened to you? Look at your shoulder.' It was all black and blue." Team physio Bill Tucker inspected the damage and Allan was quickly strapped up with Elastoplast across his left shoulder and down his body. *Wisden* was later to note that the blow to Allan's shoulder had 'destroyed his supposed value as a bowler,' but his plight seemed lost on Norman Yardley: "What do you think the bloody skipper did? He only gave me the new ball to bowl!"

Barnes and Morris opened the batting for Australia and for four overs Allan did his best, but his bowling, *The Times* observed, 'lacked both length and direction and he was accordingly hit unceremoniously by both batsmen.' "My arm was falling off. I said, 'It's no use, skipper, I can't do anything.' So I came off and Reg Simpson came on as twelfth man."

When Allan returned to the field, the first wicket was still to fall and the pitch was growing easier for batting. At 117 Hollies 'enticed Barnes just for once to grope at the ball' and Godfrey Evans pouched the catch. Allan joined with the rest of the England team as the captain called three cheers for the incoming Don Bradman. At forward short leg he had a box seat for the Don's final

Test innings. "Norman Yardley said, 'Right, Allan, as close as you like to get.' And I said, 'How close is that, skipper?' He said, 'See the whites of his eyes.' I didn't get all that close, but I saw exactly what happened to the ball." Bradman pushed forward quietly to his first delivery and Allan fielded. To Hollies' next ball, a perfectly flighted googly, Bradman lunged forward and missed. "He had the shock of his life when it bowled him! He looked down very quickly to see what the hell had happened." Had emotion finally got the better of the world's greatest run-maker? "I don't know, I can't say that," Allan replies, "but I can tell you he was dry-eyed!"

Allan remembers Bill Tucker making sure that his shoulder received urgent attention. As soon as practical he was taken off to Grosvenor Square. There he saw an Irish doctor who specialised in sports injuries. "A man called O'Flanagan, if I remember correctly. He was an Irish international rugby player and an Irish international soccer player." Allan might have added that Kevin O'Flanagan shared this unusual sporting distinction with his brother. He also played football for Arsenal and it was only the war that prevented the doctor from competing in the Olympics as a sprinter and long jumper. But, for all his medical and sporting prowess, O'Flanagan's remedy was a simple one: injections were pumped into the injured shoulder. "Then Bill Tucker came in and this doctor said, 'I don't know what else I can do. The only thing to do is to give him some more injections.' Bill said, 'How many have you given him?' 'Eight!' 'Oh Christ,' he said, 'don't give him any more.'"

After Australia's innings had closed on 389, England fared a little better in their second knock, reaching 188, but for Allan there was little to celebrate. A couple of runs saw him avoid collecting a pair before, succumbing to a Doug Ring long hop, he became the only England batsman in the match to fall to spin. "I hooked him and I thought, 'That's four runs.' But it went straight down Lindsay Hassett's throat. He didn't have to move."

In Allan's absence, Glamorgan's challenge for the Championship, thwarted by rain at Lord's, had suffered again when only eight balls could be bowled on the final day of the match against a weak Northants side at Cardiff. The home supporters then enjoyed a change of fortunes as Surrey, only four points behind Glamorgan with a game in hand at the start of the match, were routed by an innings and 24 runs, 50 year-old Johnnie Clay returning to the side to take ten wickets in the match for 66. The top of the table now read:

	Played	Points
Glamorgan	24	160
Derbyshire	25	148
Surrey	23	144
Yorkshire	23	140
Middlesex	24	136
Lancashire	24	136

This meant that the team travelled to Bournemouth knowing that one more win would put them out of reach of all other challengers, except Surrey and Yorkshire. Surrey would retain hopes for a share of the title with a draw, but Yorkshire's chance would wither should they fail to win all their remaining games. With Glamorgan's final match to be played at Leicester, where their batsmen always expected problems unravelling the left-arm mysteries of Jack Walsh, there was added pressure to complete the business in the Hampshire match.

Allan, meanwhile, could not join his team-mates on the south coast as he was required to spend a week under the care of Bill Tucker in London. "I was going to see him for treatment every morning. That's how much damage had been done to my shoulder." He stayed on with his sister Millie, anxiously wondering what was happening at Bournemouth. "I remember the chap at Hither Green station. I never stopped buying papers from him."

With Middlesex piling up the runs between the showers against Surrey at Lord's, and a blank first day for Yorkshire at Taunton, the other matches were heading in Glamorgan's direction. But the Saturday crowd at Bournemouth shared Glamorgan's frustration: they saw just ten minutes play and seven runs for their entrance money. His trips to Hither Green station brought better news for Allan on the Monday. Middlesex were heading for an innings victory over Surrey, and Somerset were frustrating Yorkshire. Meanwhile, with half-centuries from Emrys Davies, Dyson and Jones, Glamorgan's batsmen were on their way to a solid score of 315. And the runs came fast enough to give their bowlers 75 minutes to get to work that evening. By close of play the spinners were starting to wreak havoc and six Hampshire wickets had fallen for only 50.

When play resumed the next day, conditions remained helpful to spinners, and in Clay and Muncer Glamorgan had the men to make

The 1948 County Champions.
Back row (l to r): Willie Jones, Phil Clift, Jim Pleass, Allan Watkins, Hugh Griffiths, Len Muncer, Norman Hever, Gilbert Parkhouse, Jim Eaglestone. Seated (l to r): Haydn Davies, Emrys Davies, Wilfred Wooller, Arnold Dyson, George Lavis

the most of them. Hampshire's Leo Harrison remembers the carnage they wrought, as his side capsized for 94 and 116. "They were good bowlers, no doubt," he says, "but in those days batsmen were not very good at playing off spinners, thrusting their bats well in front of the pads with no give in the hands." Nine wickets in the match for the venerable Clay and seven for Muncer ensured victory by an innings and 115 runs. There were no points for Surrey and none for Yorkshire. Glamorgan were champions.

Wilf Wooller had no doubt where his team's strength lay that summer, what made it greater than the sum of its parts: "We are aware we cannot compete, for instance, with Middlesex in batting or Derbyshire in bowling. But in fielding we give first to no side." The skipper's emphasis on the importance of fielding enabled every player to feel that he was always contributing something to the team effort.

Moreover, the Glamorgan skipper also spoke of encouraging each member of his side to study tactics. "Cricket is a game requiring thought and brain. Any thinking player may see something a captain has missed. It detracts nothing from a captain's discipline to accept sound advice." Not all found it easy to make suggestions. "Wilf wasn't short in choking you off," says Allan. "Willie Jones was bloody terrified of him, and I suppose he called me a cheeky bugger. But he was a good skipper. He always spoke his mind. Of course he had a good chap with him in Haydn, but now and again there was a cross word there. Haydn would say, 'What the hell did you do that for?' or something like that."

It is nearly sixty years ago now, the day that Johnnie Clay gave vent to his feelings after the years of struggle to keep Glamorgan competing. "It seems that I am in fairyland," he is quoted as saying. Allan, too, remembers the emotions of that marvellous time as he looks back on the men who brought the title to Wales: "In the dressing room we were a noisy lot. But there was a special comradeship in the team – there's no two ways about it."

Chapter Five
South African Adventure

The County Championship coming to Wales – it had never happened before and it was a time for special celebration. Two extra matches were played, the first bringing Allan his second century of the season, when Glamorgan edged home by two wickets against a South of England XI at Swansea, and the second, against an All England XI at Cardiff, ending in a draw. That winter the players assembled for a 'family dinner' at the Dorothy Café in Cardiff and later on there was a formal reception at the City Hall. But Allan was unable to join his team-mates for either event.

Soon after the announcement of his selection for the Oval Test, he had heard that he was to be included in the MCC party for the winter's tour of South Africa. "I was so thrilled that I was picked to go to South Africa," he says, his face still lighting up as he recalls the excitement that lay ahead. The day before the Glamorgan players dined at the Dorothy, the tourists had boarded the boat train at Waterloo. A flight across the Bristol Channel with the Glamorgan team for their match with Somerset had been the nearest the young man from Usk had come to experiencing foreign travel. Now he was to be at sea for three weeks, sailing south of the equator on board the SS Durban Castle. One of the richest chapters of his life was about to open. "It was a wonderful tour. Everybody was so friendly. We were invited out everywhere. If we were in somebody's area and it was a weekend match, there'd be two or three invited out to go and have a meal there. The manager had to cut down on what people wanted us to do. I thought all touring sides were like this!"

The party of 16 was a blend of experience and younger players. With Hutton and Washbrook as established openers, Compton at number four and skipper George Mann at six, there were two batting places in the Test side to be contested between Allan, fellow left-hander Jack Crapp and two young amateurs, Reg Simpson and Charles Palmer. Though Crapp had enjoyed a good domestic season, the three younger players all owed their

The MCC party in South Africa 1948/49.
Back row (l to r): Jack Young, Roly Jenkins, Jack Crapp, Allan Watkins, Bill Ferguson (scorer),
Middle row: Godfrey Evans, Doug Wright, Cliff Gladwin, Alec Bedser, Maurice Tremlett, Reg Simpson, Charles Palmer
Front row: Brigadier M.A.Green (manager), Cyril Washbrook, Billy Griffith, George Mann (captain), Len Hutton, Denis Compton, J.Menjeits.

selection more to hunch and hope than to any weight of runs in the English summer. MCC's minutes reveal that the more experienced Jack Robertson and Arthur Fagg were standing by as batting reserves. Both could boast an average over 50 to set beside modest returns for each of the tyros: Simpson 29.18, Watkins 26.90 and Palmer 24.77.

Where Allan had felt an outsider in his first Test match, he now found he was mixing easily with the more experienced players and forging long-term friendships. "I was the youngster of the party, of course. But I was very lucky because Jack Crapp took me under his wing, and Jack Young helped me a lot. He was a great chap, and he nearly became a Glamorgan player. It was on the cards, but he decided to stay with Middlesex. We would have loved to have had him because we were short of a left-arm bowler."

Allan remembers Godfrey Evans as the clown of the party, and Denis Compton was another who became an especially good friend. "He was good to anybody, and never big-headed."

With Norman Yardley unable to tour, MCC had appointed George Mann of Middlesex as captain, and the skipper made it his business to ensure that there would be a happy atmosphere while the team would play positive cricket. "He had a way with him," says Allan. "He had a cricket brain, too, and he knew when to ask for advice. He wasn't a bad player either, certainly not a passenger."

Allan relaxes with his friends Jack Young and Jack Crapp

There were seven first-class matches before the Test series began, and Allan was chosen for four of them. At Benoni against North Eastern Transvaal he never reached the crease as he watched Denis Compton hit an amazing 300 not out in 181 minutes, but he made his case for inclusion in the first Test at Durban with 55 against Griqualand West and 61 against Transvaal. Allan had not bowled many overs, but his cause had already been strengthened by some spectacular close fielding. Palmer had failed to get going, but both Crapp and Simpson had joined the established batsmen in some heavy scoring, presenting the selectors with a tough choice to be made for the Durban Test. They decided that there would be a début for Simpson and that Allan would bat at number five.

Winning the toss, South African captain Dudley Nourse chose to bat. The openers made a nervy start and, at 18 for two, the captain joined Bruce Mitchell. South Africa's most experienced batsmen were together. They had added 51 when Allan dismissed Nourse with one of the finest catches of his life. Describing it as 'the turning point of the innings,' *Wisden* wrote: 'When Nourse placed a ball to leg, Watkins dived swiftly to his right and with one hand inches from the turf grasped the catch as he rolled over.' It is a catch, his first for England, that Allan still re-lives. He had been taught by Arnold Dyson to study each batsman closely and, noticing that Nourse pushed at Wright's googly with a strong right hand, he had asked his captain if he could move squarer. Then the catch popped up. "The amazing thing about it is that I caught the thing in my right hand. Denis was there. He said, 'Jesus Christ! Don't get up, I'll pick you up!'"

Allan's amazing catch to dismiss Dudley Nourse in the First Test at Durban

Supported by more fine catching, the two pace bowlers, Alec Bedser and Cliff Gladwin, accounted for the home team for only 161 but, when England came to bat, they soon found themselves battling on a rain-damaged pitch which dried out to provide an ideal surface for South Africa's two finger spinners, Athol Rowan and 'Tufty' Mann. With 83 from Hutton and a painstaking 72 from Compton, England led by 92 on first innings, but the leg spin of Wright and Jenkins was less well suited to the conditions and useful middle order knocks enabled South Africa to set a fourth innings target of 128.

With rain having taken its toll of the playing time, England had two hours and a quarter to score the runs, but hold ups for injury and further rain soon cost them vital minutes. This time their problems came from the pace bowlers. Operating in appalling light, but handicapped by persistent drizzle, 19-year-old Cuan McCarthy bowled superbly to take six for 43. Allan had managed only 9 on the turning pitch in the first innings. Now he came in with the score at 52 for three and he had made only 4 when he was bowled by McCarthy, to be followed in quick succession by Simpson, who had dropped down the order, and Evans. Catches had already been missed in the gathering gloom before Compton and Jenkins added 43 crucial runs; but both were out before the final eight-ball over was reached with South Africa needing two wickets while England required eight runs.

Bedser and Gladwin were at the wicket, neither a specialist batsman, with only Wright to come. As Lindsay Tuckett came in to bowl, Allan was no longer able to watch. "Denis and I were down in the toilets," he admits. After a single to Bedser, an agricultural heave by Gladwin eluded Eric Rowan, who had crept in from the boundary. Another single to fine leg was followed by two dot balls, then Bedser scampered through to level the scores. Gladwin was now back on strike but the next ball passed him down the leg side. "They've got to run whatever happens," John Arlott told listeners back in Britain, as Tuckett prepared to deliver the final ball. And run they did as the ball cannoned into Gladwin's thigh, Bedser just making his ground before the wicket could be broken. Allan was still in the toilets. "The roar went up and we knew we had won." He had taken part in what remains the only Test match ever to have been won off the last available ball.

The second Test at Ellis Park, Johannesburg was to start on 27 December. MCC's minutes record that 'it was decided to send Christmas cards to the wives of members of the MCC party.' More important for the wives, no doubt, was the clause in their husbands' contracts that permitted one free telephone call home, at the festive season. His team-mates would later envy Allan a second chance to speak with his wife when he sat in the control tower at Durban Airport to join in a St David's Day broadcast in which Molly and Wilf Wooller spoke to Welsh listeners worldwide.

Allan and Reg Simpson had contributed little with the bat in the first Test, but, helped by his fielding, Allan retained his place, while the young amateur made way for the more experienced Jack Crapp, when the side was chosen for Johannesburg. An opening stand of 359 between Hutton and Washbrook set a new world record for Test matches, and Compton was also approaching three figures when Allan joined him at 516 for three. For a while he was content to play second fiddle, but after Compton's dismissal the remaining wickets fell quickly, Allan's among them for just 7. There were two more catches for Allan, the one that accounted for Dawson taking the headlines back in Wales, and his first Test wicket came when Tuckett was stumped by Evans. Following on 293 in arrears but in conditions still favourable to the bat, South Africa's second innings was notable for an unbeaten 156 from Eric Rowan, who had already been dropped from the side for the third Test of the series, but who now steered his country to safety.

With the Cape Town Test starting just two days later, on the beautiful Newlands ground, the players broke with tradition by flying from Johannesburg. England again won the toss and chose to bat. They had reached 151 for three when Allan joined Washbrook. When the Lancashire batsman was immediately out, there was a need to retrench. Helping his captain add 51, Allan batted usefully to reach 27, his first double figure score in six Test starts, and England were glad to reach 308. The South Africans replied with 356, their innings built around centuries by Mitchell and Nourse. Yet, with Mitchell's 120 taking 344 minutes, England never truly surrendered the initiative. By the close of the third day, with only Washbrook out, they led by 37 runs.

Making the game safe was the first priority when Hutton and Crapp resumed next day but, though his side were one up in the series, George Mann still determined that he would push for victory. He took Allan to one side before he went in. "'I haven't told Denis,' he said, 'but we're going to declare.' So I went in and said, 'Denis, you'd better get on with it.' He was about five when I went in, but I beat him to his fifty. Coming off, he came up to me, 'You bloody Welsh bastard!' he said. That's what he always called me!" Allan had gone to the wicket with his future as a Test player in the balance, but he played his strokes with freedom, his undefeated 64 taking just 103 minutes and containing nine fours. Mann's declaration set South Africa to make 229 in 125 minutes, but their batsmen could not be tempted.

Following the leisurely pattern of tours in the early post-war years, there were five provincial matches before MCC returned to Johannesburg for the fourth Test. A pitch less accommodating to the bat had been prepared by the Ellis Park ground staff, but England were still glad to bat first. Washbrook was again in good form, but he succumbed to a catch on the fine leg boundary for 97 shortly after Allan had joined him. Mann soon followed and, with the score on 213 for five, the South Africans were well placed. Allan had settled in, but now he had only the lower order for company. Finding a useful partner in Jenkins, he steered England to 290 for seven at the close, his own score 64.

Next day, after surviving an early chance on the leg side, Allan found support from Gladwin, and then Griffith, Evans' replacement as wicket-keeper, but when Griffith was ninth man out, Allan's score stood on 91. "I remember Jack Young coming in. 'Don't worry. I'll be there till the end,' he said. I was anxious. It was my first century in Test cricket and I was dreading getting out on 96 or something." Declining two singles to retain the strike, Allan prolonged the wait before he finally turned Tuckett to the leg-side boundary. Shortly after, he trod on his stumps as the innings closed on 379. "I remember Jack ribbing me that I was the one who had got out." Lusty hooks and pulls had been a feature of Allan's 111, which contained 15 fours.

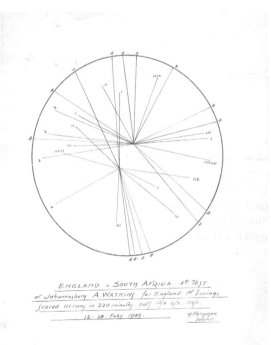

The wagon wheel of Allan's century, an early example of Bill Ferguson's craft, which shows Allan's strength square of the wicket.

Allan returned to well deserved applause. "I walked towards the dressing room," he recalls, "and the first person who met me was Cyril Washbrook. Cyril said 'I hope that's the first of many.' Then I walked into the dressing room and Len Hutton was sat there. He said, 'If you don't cut out that bloody hook shot, you won't get any runs on a Sunday afternoon.' That was Len Hutton's congratulations for me getting my first hundred in Test matches!"

Allan's innings, followed by the early loss of prime South African wickets, gave England control of the match. Once again Mann's declaration failed to tempt batsmen for whom survival was their dominant priority throughout the series, though Allan picked up a couple of top order wickets in the fourth innings. So England came to the final Test at Port Elizabeth knowing that they could not lose the series. The tourists were still undefeated in all matches but, replying to South Africa's 379, it was only thanks to an unbeaten 136 by their popular captain that they avoided following on and eventually led by 16 on first innings.

South Africa's batsmen had once again lacked enterprise, and they had still shown surprisingly little urgency in their second innings when Nourse made a belated gesture to square the series. His declaration set England to make 172 in 95 minutes. Such challenges were rarely accepted by teams not needing to win, but Mann determined to have a go. The early batsmen set off at a cracking pace, but wickets soon began to fall. Allan, held back with Crapp to shore up the innings should things go wrong, found his nerves tested to the limit. Usually a chain smoker as he waited to bat, he recalls talking in the dressing room with Compton: "I said 'Are you ever nervous, Denis?' He said, 'What do you think this is?' His hand was shaking like a leaf! He said, 'People who tell you they're not nervous going in to bat are not worth a candle.'"

At 153 for seven, as Allan went in to join Crapp, 19 runs were still required with ten minutes remaining. "I asked the skipper for instructions before I walked to the wicket," Allan later told a reporter, "And he said, 'Do your best to stay there, but try and get the runs.'" With Allan working the strike for his partner, ten were needed as Mann began what might have been the final eight-ball over. There were three singles then Crapp 'smote three times with the power of a blacksmith'. Four, two, four – and the match was won with a minute to spare with what were to be Jack Crapp's last strokes in Test cricket.

The dramatic win at Port Elizabeth set the seal on a wonderful tour. Wherever the team had gone they had been fêted. Amid much fine cricket, they had found time to visit Victoria Falls, to travel the Garden Route and to admire the views from the top of Table Mountain.

Allan prepares to drive off

For many of the party, Allan among them, there had been the chance to enjoy a first taste of golf, and there was much merriment out on the course with the likes of Jack Young. "I remember we were coming past the clubhouse and Jack sliced his ball straight through the window of a car. I thought 'What's going to happen now?' Then the fellow who owned the car came out and he said, 'I enjoyed that. Now I'll go and put a new windscreen in,' he said. 'Fancy my car being hit by an MCC player!'"

The team had enjoyed five months away from the ration-book austerity of post-war Britain and, as a gesture from a more prosperous nation, the Johannesburg Food Parcels Committee sent to the home towns of each of the players 100 food parcels each weighing six pounds. The Usk consignment went with a special message that one should go to Mrs Watkins, and most of the town's older inhabitants benefited from the South Africans' generosity.

In similarly grateful mood, the South African Cricket Association awarded each of the tourists a bonus of £75. MCC were a bit huffy about this gesture, which had been made without seeking their approval. Minutes of the Cricket Committee record concern lest the amateurs, provided with a tour allowance of just £150, should have their amateur status imperilled and, for the professionals, there was to be a warning that they should all realise that the money would be taxed at nine shillings [45p] in the pound!

Chapter Six
Back on the County Circuit

There was a regal welcome back to Usk. One of young Allen's earliest memories is of the crowds thronging Twyn Square for the return of his father, a father of whom all his children say they saw so little for months on end. Soon Allan was preparing to start another season with Glamorgan. With an average of 35.85 in the Tests and his reputation as a fielder reinforced on the international stage, he had hopes of cementing a place in the Test side. His bowling may have played a part in securing his place at the start of the winter tour, but with only 96 first-class overs and just four wickets, all of them in the Tests, it was principally as a batsman that he needed to state his case.

The resignation of Johnnie Clay as a selector may have cost Allan some support, but he remained high on the list of possibles for a place in the Tests against New Zealand. He might have helped his cause had he opened the new season with a bang, but he failed to prosper on the early season pitches in Wales. Chosen for MCC against the tourists at Lord's in May, he managed a hard earned 69, but a duck in the first innings of the Test trial opened the door to other batsmen. Bill Edrich, who had been unable to tour South Africa, regained his place and a first cap was given to another young left-hander, Alan Wharton of Lancashire, who had opened the season with a succession of big scores.

When Wharton, who had failed in the first Test, pulled out of the second at Lord's, Allan was summoned to deputise. An undefeated 49 in the second innings went some way to offsetting a first innings failure but, by the time he came out to bat, the match was already dead, a victim of MCC wrongly assuming that the New Zealanders would not be worthy of four-day matches, a decision that was to condemn all four of the summer's Tests to stalemate.

Wholesale changes for the third Test meant that Allan was one of five who had played at Lord's to be omitted from the team for Old Trafford. New faces were coming into the England side, and Allan would have to wait three years before playing his next Test on home soil. In what was to become a summer of disappointment, he missed selection for the Gentlemen and Players match at Lord's and, despite four championship centuries, he batted inconsistently with lean periods bereft of runs, though his bowling brought some compensation with 66 first-class wickets. Meanwhile, Glamorgan slipped to eighth place in the table, the warm dry weather bringing the 1948 champions twice as many drawn games.

After MCC had sent parties overseas for three consecutive winters, no tour was scheduled for 1949/50; so Allan reported for duty with Cardiff City, as he had expected to do twelve months earlier. His selection for South Africa had brought only good wishes from his new club. When he had spoken to H.H.Merrett, any concerns about a clash of commitments were swept aside. "He said, 'No choice at all – South Africa for you! I'm thrilled because I'm chairman of Cardiff City and I've got one of my boys playing for England.'" When Allan returned he had found an unexpected and welcome surprise at the football club: "Every week HH had paid my wages into the safe. I thought it was wonderful."

Now it was time for Allan to repay his employer's generosity, and he had plenty to offer. "Allan was a good footballer," says brother Selwyn, who won countless cups as a teenager with Usk before going on to a professional career with Bath City, Bristol City and other clubs. "Perhaps a bit slow, but very good at reading the game. He has a very acute brain when it comes to sport."

Keeping his weight in check was always a problem for Allan, especially in the summer months, so there was work to do in the sweat baths when he reported for duty with Cardiff City. Then he captained a side in the Welsh Cup at Merthyr Tydfil. "The ground was pretty rough there. I tossed up and went back to left half, where I was playing. Their inside right doubled back and I went to double back with him, caught my foot in one of these tufts of ruddy grass and my cartilage went. So I was on the field about twenty seconds, I think, before I was carried off." This was Allan's second cartilage to go, rugby having claimed the first. An operation for the removal of the cartilage was successfully carried out, but Allan was told that his career as a footballer was at an end. He would never step onto the field for a full Cardiff City side.

Allan saw the club secretary. "He said, 'You've got a broken contract. H.H. wants to know how much you want for it.' I said, 'How much do *I* want?' He said, 'It's worth a thousand or two thousand pounds.' So I said, 'Where's that contract?' He said, 'It's in the safe.' I said, 'Get it out and give it to me.' He gave it to me and I tore it up. He said, 'What the hell have you done? You're a bit of a bloody fool.' I said, 'No, I'm not. Because when I went to South Africa, all my pay packets were in the safe when I came back.'"

Returning to cricket in 1950, Allan enjoyed an improved season with the bat, raising his average from 30 to just over 40, but the after-effects of his operation prevented him from bowling in the early matches and he sent down barely half the overs of the previous summer. Glamorgan, meanwhile, dropped further down the table, now victims of an exceptionally wet summer in which nine championship matches were abandoned without a decision on first innings.

In the eyes of the not always objective J.B.G.Thomas, writing in *Playfair*, Allan was 'unlucky not to go to Australia'. Despite the wet summer, his form had certainly been better than in 1949, but he

West Indian opener Allan Rae bowled by Allan for 11 at Swansea

had seen a succession of new players winning Test caps. Reg Simpson had come in for the third Test against New Zealand, when Brian Close played for the first time, and that summer had seen the emergence of Trevor Bailey, first chosen to spearhead the attack but also capable of making useful runs. Against West Indies in 1950, other new batsmen were tried, a disproportionate number – Doggart, Dewes, Insole and Sheppard – following in Bailey's footsteps from Cambridge. That winter, another Light Blue, fast bowler John Warr, was chosen to tour Australia, in a party travelling under the captaincy of Freddie Brown, yet another Cambridge man, though of an earlier vintage.

To those in the professional ranks, the whiff of nepotism hung around the corridors of Lord's. For the likes of Allan it felt as though there was a conspiracy against them. Brown, it was said, insisted on taking the party of his choice to Australia, but critics felt that the team's prospects had been reduced before they set sail by some of the selections. In the event, Warr, Hollies and Berry achieved little as bowlers, while the quartet of inexperienced batsmen – Dewes, Sheppard, Close and Allan's Glamorgan team-mate Gilbert Parkhouse – were all found wanting.

With professional football behind him, Allan decided to spend the winter in South Africa, where there was a long tradition of Glamorgan players taking up coaching positions. It was the veteran opening batsman Emrys Davies, the county's senior professional, who first suggested that Allan might enjoy the experience. Emrys and the pre-war player Dai Davies, now a Test umpire, were planning to make their annual trip to South Africa. The quiet, deeply religious Emrys would be heading for Kimberley, while Dai was going to Johannesburg, where Allan would accompany him.

In Johannesburg Allan and Dai divided their time between several secondary schools, and twice a week they had to cope with a hundred boys of differing ages and ability at Ellis Park. Among those chosen to attend was a lanky 14-year-old in whose future Allan would soon show a paternal interest. Peter Walker, destined to be on the Glamorgan staff for 18 years and to play three Tests for England, had first come across Allan when he had toured two years earlier. Now describing him as "my mentor", the young Walker had been in Durban to see Allan catching Dudley Nourse. "It stuck in my memory," he says years later, "as Nourse was the big hero of South African batting. I can't remember the shot. I just remember this fat figure diving to the right in his white sun hat and catching it."

During that tour, Allan had taken up an introduction offered by Les Spence, at one time honorary secretary at Glamorgan, and called on Spence's old friend Oliver Walker, Peter's father. A former leader writer for the *Western Mail*, Walker senior had emigrated to South Africa, where he was a much respected literary editor of *The Star* in Johannesburg and would later become an outspoken opponent of the apartheid system, more than once offering his home as a clandestine meeting place for the young, still little-known Nelson Mandela.

This was the home to which Allan had come round for dinner, bringing with him a still treasured memento for young Peter Walker – the dirty old sun hat in which he had taken the catch which had made such a lasting impression on the young boy in the crowd at Durban. Peter owes much to Allan, an early advocate that he should cut his pace as a bowler and, crucially, the man who first implanted the Glamorgan creed that fielding wins matches.

*Allan catches Jack Cheetham off Jim McConnon
in Glamorgan's dramatic victory against the South Africans at Swansea.*

As he would find in later life, Allan, with his thoughtful and analytical approach to the game, and his passion for it, had a gift for coaching. However, the trip to South Africa was not repeated. It meant a winter away from his family, and it was not the financial success he had hoped. "It could have been worth it," he reflects, "if I had been like Dai, because Dai never moved out of the pub where we both lived. He was a homely sort of a chap. He just sat in the bar. He never went to the pictures or anything. But I had friends in Johannesburg and I used to go out and see them."

With the off spinners of Jim McConnon adding a new bite to the attack, Glamorgan rose to fifth in the table in 1951 and had the distinction of becoming the only county to beat the South Africans that summer. This match was memorable for the bowling of Muncer and McConnon, who spun the tourists to a 64-run defeat, claiming all ten second innings wickets for only 29 more runs after the opening pair had added 54. For Allan the match brought back memories of his catch to dismiss Nourse at Durban: "Dudley loved playing the ball off his pads and he came to Swansea and I'm damned if I didn't do him again." Among Allan's five catches in the match he twice snapped up Nourse off the bowling of Muncer.

Chapter Seven
Senior Professional in India

Allan had enjoyed a good all-round season in 1951 with 1,620 runs, 64 wickets and 40 catches. It was enough to win him a place in the MCC team for the tour of India, Pakistan and Ceylon. All the leading players preferred to take a winter's rest and only two of the party, Roy Tattersall and Brian Statham, had been on the tour of Australia, the Lancashire pair having flown out as reinforcements. When Jack Ikin withdrew in favour of Cyril Poole, only nine of the 16 setting off for India had played Test cricket and only Tattersall, with nine, had more than Allan's seven caps.

Nigel Howard, Lancashire's 26-year-old captain, was chosen to lead the team. The last of the mandatory amateurs plucked optimistically from county cricket, Howard had as his vice-captain Donald Carr, a former captain of Oxford University, soon to take over at Derbyshire. A third amateur was wicket-keeper Don Brennan of Yorkshire. Lancashire also provided the manager, their secretary Geoffrey Howard, unrelated to the captain, taking on single-handed a range of jobs that would now be shared by an army of assistants. Allan travelled as senior professional and, with a young captain who was hardly up to the job, it taxed him to the full. "I had to do a lot of thinking and talking," he admits.

An arduous trip lay ahead, a letter from MCC to the Indian Board showing some awareness of what might be in store in a country still finding its feet after Partition:

> 'We have heard most alarming rumours of the present problems facing Europeans travelling by rail in India and feel that all journeys should be by air (or possibly road) except for a night journey leaving after dinner and arriving at its destination before breakfast. In particular, we regard the rail journey from Calcutta to Kanpur and thence to Nagpur as being objectionable.'

Anticipating a quite different set of problems, another pre-tour missive was sent to the Board:

'We agree to the luncheon interval of 60 minutes and tea interval of 15 minutes provided we are assured that there will be no speeches in the luncheon interval at any of the Tests.'

MARYLEBONE CRICKET CLUB.

CUN. 2241

Lord's Cricket Ground,

London, N.W.8.

July 20. 1951

Dear Sir,

I am directed by the M.C.C. Committee to ask your Committee if they will allow *A. Watkins* to join the M.C.C. Team which will visit India, Pakistan and Ceylon in 1951/52.

The Team will sail on Tuesday, September 18th, 1951 in s.s. "Chusan" from Tilbury.

Should your Committee agree, would you kindly hand the enclosed invitation to *A. Watkins* and let us know as soon as possible whether he will accept the invitation and if so on what date it would be convenient for him to be medically examined by Dr. R.B.D. Wright, 7, Warwick Avenue, W.9. M.C.C. will then make an appointment and pay the fees for the medical examination.

Will you please complete and return to me the enclosed medical history sheet in respect of *A. Watkins*

The terms and conditions on which an invitation is issued are embodied in the enclosed agreement, a copy of which will be forwarded to each professional for signature.

Yours faithfully,

R. Aird.

Secretary, M.C.C.

The Secretary

Glamorgan C.C.C

Molly travelled to London to see the party off on the boat train from St Pancras. From Tilbury they sailed to Bombay. They had left behind the reassurance of home cooking as a variety of different arrangements were made for their accommodation - hotels with only basic comforts, private homes and state guest houses. "And maharajahs' palaces with no water," Tom Graveney adds, going on to recall the drink restrictions: "We had to sign the forms to show we were all alcoholics and needed 28 bottles of beer and four bottles of whisky to last for a month. And we pooled all this stuff and carted it round with us."

Donald Carr had been in India as a boy, and Dick Spooner and Fred Ridgway had toured with a Commonwealth side the previous winter, but the rest of the party were new to the sub-continental conditions. They were soon tested by the intense heat and challenged by the alien and ever-changing playing conditions. It seemed that there were never two surfaces the same: "Turf, coconut mats, jute mats," says Tom Graveney, "but they made sure we never played on a turf pitch before a Test!"

Their first match was in Bombay and they went on to play at Ahmedabad, Indore, Amritsar and Dehra Dun before arriving in New Delhi for the first Test. After five matches they were still unbeaten but had managed only one win, scrambling home by two wickets on coir matting against Western India at Ahmedabad.

On a pitch expected to suit his style of bowling, they entered the Test without leg-spinner Bert Rhodes, who had already returned home with a rumbling appendix, and then, on the eve of the match, Tom Graveney, who had been in prime form, went down with dysentery. It was not a promising start. Nigel Howard won the toss

The guest house at Indore

but, once the leg breaks and googlies of Shinde were introduced to the attack, his team were in trouble. Allan, who had not shown much form in the early matches, contributed a useful 40 to a disappointing total of 203, *Wisden* reporting that 'hitting with the spin, Watkins was the only batsman to play the leg-spinner well.' India's batsmen then ground their way to 418 for six as first Merchant, with 154, then Hazare, with an unbeaten 164, claimed the record for their country's highest individual score. After a rest day, England began their second innings 215 behind with two full days left for play.

With Mankad's left-arm spin soon in operation in support of Shinde, England's batsmen dug in. Jack Robertson helped Frank Lowson add 61 before falling to Mankad and, on the stroke of lunch, Shinde dismissed Don Kenyon. Allan had batted at number five in the first innings, but now he moved up the order. "I remember the manager coming in. He said, 'We'd better send a left-hander in.' So Dick Spooner came up and said, 'I'll go in.' I said, 'You bloody well won't. I'm the senior professional on this tour – I'm the boss.' So I went in."

By close of play England had lost Lowson, but Allan and Donald Carr stood firm. They had added 86, but at 202 for three they had still to wipe out the deficit. Next day the stand continued and the pair had been together five hours when Carr, who had survived two chances, finally edged Shinde to slip for 76. "Allan kept me going," he says. "I like to think that I kept him going a bit too. I'd never batted five hours in my life. Never did afterwards, I don't think."

Spooner soon followed and, when Howard was all at sea against Shinde, Allan declined singles to prevent his captain facing the leg spinner. He remained on 98 for 20 minutes and spent another ten on 99 before pulling Shinde to the boundary. His century had taken seven hours and 20 minutes. Shortly before the tea interval, Howard's charmed life ended, but after nearly an hour at the crease he had helped stretch the lead to 94. The Indians were into the tail, but time was running out for them. Allan's job in the searing heat was nearly done.

"Derek Shackleton came in. He said, 'Right, Allan, you do the shouting.' I hit a ball to square leg and I went to run two, but I couldn't pick my bloody feet up. So I only ran one. I said to Derek, 'You stay that end and I'll stay this end.' We must have batted about three quarters of an hour and I scored about three runs. I was finished, I couldn't run. My legs were gone completely." Donald Carr recalls Allan saying that once the game was safe he was going to give the leg spinner 'some terrible clout'. But, when the time came, "he couldn't reach mid off. He was absolutely exhausted and he'd lost his timing for hitting the ball."

Allan had batted for nine hours without giving a chance for an undefeated 137, 'a glorious innings which undoubtedly saved England.' Contemporary record books credit him with 138, but later corrections have passed one run to Shackleton. Perhaps the players were not the only ones overcome by the heat.

There were echoes of what might now be a man of the match award. Allan was recovering in the showers when a message came through. "Somebody said, 'There's a man outside wants to see you, Allan.' I went outside and someone gave me a little plaque out on the balcony. I hadn't a clue who he was. He just gave it to me and walked away. I can't remember his name now, but I've still got it somewhere."

From Delhi the team flew to Pakistan, where they were to play five matches, two of them branded unofficial 'Tests' in a country still to be awarded full status. The players departed leaving their luggage in the care of the manager. Geoffrey Howard, meanwhile, set off by train for Amritsar, where he transferred 38 pieces of baggage into a three-ton army truck to complete the journey to the border and into a country whose Prime Minister had been assassinated only a few weeks earlier.

The team were growing used to the rigours of travel on the sub-continent. They made many of their journeys in twin-engined Dakotas, quite often with the tour manager taking the controls. 'The chaps are always jittery when I take over, but it is as safe as it can be at 8,000 feet!' Geoffrey Howard wrote to his wife, adding reassuringly, 'with the pilot at my side with dual controls.'

'Expecting a reasonably quiet time in Pakistan, MCC found the standard of cricket higher than anticipated,' wrote *Wisden* after the first 'Test' at Lahore, where an unbroken stand of 259 by Graveney and Spooner in the second innings rescued the tourists. From Lahore to Bahawalpur they travelled by train, conforming to MCC's wish that such journeys should be made only at night. For the amateurs it was pleasant enough in their air-conditioned coach. "The locals made the arrangements for the team," Donald

Carr explains, "and the amateurs were in first class and the pros were in second class. We thought it a bit off, but it was rather funny. We had a rather nice couchette area and quite a good meal and settled down for the night. We hoped the boys were all right, but we didn't check up too carefully."

Passing through desert on its way, the train arrived next morning at Bahawalpur. Donald Carr and his fellow amateurs had passed a comfortable night. "We were brought a cup of tea and I said to Geoffrey, 'Shall I let the troops out now?' We turned out in our smart blazers and hats – we always wore hats to look the part – and I went down to the truck at the back. There facing me as I pulled the doors open was Allan absolutely covered in red dust, his little eyes peering out. I said, 'Come on, are you all right?' He said, 'It's all right for you f——g amateurs!' I roared with laughter. I said, 'You're getting paid, Watty! We're amateurs.' It lasted about a week, his anger. It's almost my favourite recollection of Watty."

The journey to Karachi ahead of the second 'Test', as Allan recounts it, gave the players different reasons for concern: "We went in one of those old cargo planes. The pilot took us down and we went in to land at the ordinary airport, but they wouldn't let us down. So we had to go to their RAF airfield. We went wobbling across Karachi and when we came down we finished up facing the wrong way. The plane went round on its wheels after landing. The poor old pilot wouldn't come back. They usually came back and we thanked them, but he wouldn't come back. We learnt later that it was the first time the poor bugger had flown at night."

Entering their final match in Pakistan, the tourists were fortunate to have their unbeaten record intact. Soon it would be challenged. The first 'Test' in Lahore had been played on a beautiful turf pitch, but now they were back on coconut matting. "It was a hard shale strip with the mat on top," says Tom Graveney, "and depending on whether they were batting or fielding they loosened the mat." "I remember that," says Allan. "It was my job to make sure they rolled it properly." Graveney top scored with 19 as England were skittled for 123. "Fazal Mahmood made the ball talk," he says. "He bowled medium-paced cutters and bounced it both ways." Good bowling by Statham and Shackleton restricted the first innings deficit to just seven, after which a splendid century by Graveney set Pakistan 285 to win. With the umpires turning down every appeal for lbw, a 16-year-old Hanif Mohammad paved the way to victory, which came by four wickets, reinforcing the host country's claims to Test status.

"He was a good player, young Hanif," says Allan. "He was such a quiet unassuming batsman, but he played his shots. There was nothing hurried, there was no forcing it. He wasn't a big man, but he was a beautiful player."

Back in Bombay for the second Test against India, Allan, as senior professional, sat down with the captain, vice-captain and manager to choose the side. A ticklish problem confronted them. Graveney was now fit and an automatic choice as a batsman. But who should make way? The opening pair were settled, Kenyon had just run into form and the other batting places were taken by the heroes of the Delhi Test, Allan and Donald Carr. It was Allan who spoke up: "Well I think the

Allan bowling on another unresponsive Indian pitch

skipper is the natural person to leave out." This was awkward advice for the young captain, but it was a problem that had been anticipated before the team left England. Nigel Howard had been firmly told to make sure he played regardless of form. In an unhappy compromise Carr was omitted. "I think it was reasonable that Nigel should play," he now says. "I probably didn't think so at the time!"

A second change saw the replacement of Shackleton by Eddie Leadbeater. There had been great determination to get another leg spinner to replace Rhodes. An urgent cable to MCC had drawn a disappointing response:

'Jenkins, Wright, Hollies, Lawrence not available STOP Appleyard available. Would you like him or any other? STOP Cable or telephone as convenient.'

Bob Appleyard had taken 200 wickets for Yorkshire that summer, but the tourists were determined to have another leg spinner, so it was Eddie Leadbeater, with only 81 wickets, who flew out to join them. After just one match he was thrust into the Test side as a spinner ahead of Malcolm Hilton, who had been in the party from the outset. Leadbeater bowled only 11 overs as India piled up 485 for nine, while Allan sent down 32. "I was over-bowled on that tour," he says. "Because they made me a stock bowler and I bowled for hour after hour while Fred Ridgway and Brian Statham were resting. In those conditions – I was just above medium – I had to rely completely on what happened off the pitch."

Tom Graveney batting in his long partnership with Allan in the Second Test at Bombay.

For containing the Indians to a lead of 29, England were indebted to Tom Graveney, whose 175 was a monument of patience. Allan, with 80, helped him add 148 for the fifth wicket. His long innings over, Allan picked up the valuable wickets of Hazare and Amarnath on the fourth evening as India collapsed to 42 for four. Next day he bowled Mankad to finish with three for 20, his best return in Tests, but the Indian lower order resisted till a run chase was no longer a serious proposition for England's batsmen.

Yet another draw, against Maharastra at Poona, was followed by an innings victory against Bengal, where Allan made a hard-hit 113 not out, ahead of the third Test at Eden Gardens in Calcutta. This brought another dreary draw on a lifeless pitch, Allan maintaining his consistent form with a patient 68 when England were on the brink of collapse. He later rose from a sick bed, shrugging aside a sore throat, to bowl a long and economical spell when a jarred knee had forced Statham from the field. Allan was in the runs again with 63 in a nine-wicket victory against East Zone, as the tour moved on to the fourth Test at Kanpur.

For the first time England now found a pitch to suit their finger spinners. Tattersall and Hilton, making his first appearance of the series, dismissed India for 121. Runs continued at a premium when England batted, as the off spinner Ghulam Ahmed and left-armer Mankad enjoyed the conditions, but Allan's splendid run continued. Helping England to a lead of 82, he top-scored with 66, while none of his colleagues could make more than 21.

When India batted a second time it was Hilton who made the early inroads. Somehow wickets eluded Tattersall, and nothing seemed to be going England's way as Adhikari and Umrigar settled in to a stubborn sixth wicket partnership. Allan remembers the captain turning to him for advice. "'What would you do Allan?' I said, 'Put Jack Robertson on.' He said, 'He doesn't bowl.' I said, 'Put him on!' So Jack took a wicket – Polly Umrigar. Nigel said, 'Well done, Allan. That's marvellous.' I said, 'Now take him off!' He said, 'What?' I said 'Take him off and put Roy back on.' Because Jack was just a roller, he wasn't an off spinner and Roy was a bloody good bowler but nothing was happening for him. He went back on and won the match for us."

MCC won two of their next three zonal matches and came to the final Test at Madras in good heart. They had beaten South Zone with ten minutes to spare, but their captain had not been in

Bangalore to witness it. Nigel Howard, who had never taken to India and always feared for his health, had developed pleurisy and was in a nursing home. He was still on the sick list when the Test started and Donald Carr deputised.

Carr won the toss and England batted, but they could manage only 266 as Vinoo Mankad, with eight for 55, became the first Indian to take eight wickets in a Test match innings. The death of King George VI caused the rest day to be brought forward, after which Roy and Umrigar both hit centuries, enabling India to declare on 457 for nine. England's batsmen were then bowled out for 183, Robertson with a second fifty in what would be his last Test match and Allan, with 48, the only batsmen to resist. Donald Carr reflects on the loss of his only Test as captain, a defeat that brought India their first Test match victory: "The newspapers said that the local Indians didn't expect us to play too well because of the death of the king, which was very nice of them. But I don't know whether it made very much difference. We were a bit tired, I think, and they were a better side than us."

On they went for three more weeks in Ceylon, the modern Sri Lanka. The better appointed hotels were welcome to the tourists, but there was a rude awakening on the field when they found that their first opponents, a Commonwealth XI, included Keith Miller, Neil Harvey and five other established Test players. A century from Miller followed by early wickets in each innings on a juicy pitch consigned MCC to an innings defeat. Allan remembers Miller setting the tone by knocking Jack Robertson's cap off in his first over. "When we'd spoken to Keith in the hotel the night before he'd said, 'Don't worry, I shan't be trying too hard.' He was trying as hard as he could! But we got our own back." The revenge came in the next match as the tourists' pride was restored with an even more emphatic victory over the full Ceylon side, but Allan, now exhausted, bowled eight wicketless overs and scored just 2.

With only two more two-day games before they caught the boat for home, Allan and Jack Robertson were given a well earned rest, enabling them to visit a tea plantation in the mountains. The manager gave them time off on one condition: "He said, 'You're skippering the side at Galle, so Nigel Howard and Donald Carr can have a rest.' I said, 'Yes.' Then he said, 'By the way I'm playing!'" Geoffrey Howard played in both matches, acquitting himself well for a one-time club cricketer whose last serious match had been before the war.

Allan can look back on five long months travelling the length and breadth of the sub-continent. He had played in 19 of the 23 first-class matches - only Graveney and Robertson, neither of them all-rounders, had played as many. "It was a hell of a hard tour. I know I'm getting old and decrepit, but what would they do today? They'd all break down by the morning." They had endured all manner of discomfort and put up with endless civic functions but, though there had been no coaches, masseurs or baggage men, their daily chores had been eased by having personal bearers at their disposal. For other members of the team one bearer was shared between two but, as senior professional, Allan had one to himself. "We were lucky to have them," he says. "Your clothes got soaking wet after every session. They couldn't have done better for us."

"Watty was a lovely man," says Donald Carr. "He kept us going. A dedicated sort of chap with some Test and tour experience, and I think we needed it. The amateurs were all pretty inexperienced." Tom Graveney echoes his vice-captain's thoughts: "He was a marvellous senior pro, Allan. A lovely man, and a very good cricketer. Everybody respected him and took his advice. I remember in the first match of the tour I'd made a hundred in the first innings and I didn't want to go in again – let someone else have a knock. Allan had a quiet word: 'You go in where you're told,' he said. So I had to get my pads on!"

Leslie Smith, writing in *Wisden*, says of Allan on this tour that 'his Test average of 64.42 was the best for either side and India feared him more than anyone else. His grim determination and fighting spirit were a joy to behold.' In 1952, the magazine *Indian Cricket* made him one of its five Cricketers of the Year, for his performances in the Tests, the only English player to be so recognised in that Indian season. In modern parlance, he was the 'Player of the Series' for England.

Chapter Eight
The Best All-Rounder in English Cricket

Molly was at the quayside when the tourists arrived back at Tilbury. Their ship docked late, and she and Joyce Robertson, Jack's wife, had to endure a bitterly cold March night before they were re-united with their husbands in the morning. By evening Molly and Allan were back at 'Ellis Park', the home to which they had moved in the Ladysmith area of Usk and which they had named after the ground on which Allan had hit his first Test century.

The returning hero looked fit and well, but throughout his career Allan lived on his nerves and never more so than after the long months in India. "It was a good trip," he says, "but mind you I suffered for it afterwards." Allan remembers a conversation with Molly not long after his return. "I said to her, 'Someone told me I was going round the twist.' She said, 'You are! You haven't sat down to a decent meal with me and the children since you came back from India. You're always up and about.' And of course she was right. And I knew I was dreaming. I threw my hand out one night and made her nose bleed. She said I was saying, 'Catch the bloody thing!' So that's how it affected me in the long run."

There was a month's break to restore the shattered nerves before the domestic season got under way and a rare chance for a holiday with the family, which now included daughter Judith. As they set off by car to revisit old haunts at Plymouth and spend some time in Cornwall, Allan had plenty on which to ponder after his winter tour. No batsman on either side had scored more than his 450 runs in the Tests. Might he now retain a place in the England team for the summer when, by a curious quirk of planning, the Indians would be touring England?

Despite the recall of most of the established players who had wintered at home, the two batting successes from India, Tom Graveney and Allan, both found places in the eleven for the first Test at Leeds. They were to bat at five and six in a side to be captained by Len Hutton. Appointing a professional for the first time since MCC had assumed responsibility for selection was the big talking point. Another was their choice of a new fast bowler, Fred Trueman, to open the attack with Bedser.

Though England would soon dominate opponents who lacked resolution against Trueman's raw pace, the series began well for the visitors. After making 293, they held the whip hand as Ghulam Ahmed exploited helpful conditions to reduce England to 92 for four. At this point Allan joined Graveney. Together they added 90, Allan's share 48. For *Wisden* their gritty batting was 'the turning point of the match'. A sparkling innings from Evans helped England to a first innings lead of 41, after which the Indians made the worst start to an innings in Test history. Four batsmen dismissed, three of them to Trueman, without a run in the book spelt the end of any serious challenge, England easing home by eight wickets.

For the Lord's Test the Indians gained the release of Vinoo Mankad from his Lancashire League commitments to Haslingden. Scoring 72 and 184, and bowling 73 overs to take five wickets, he did all in his power to keep India in the game, but it was to no avail. England's batsmen filled their boots, Hutton leading the way with 150, but poor Allan was bowled by Mankad for a duck just before

Allan meets the Queen at the Lord's Test in 1952.

close of play on the second day. He had made his main contribution earlier in the match, first holding a fine catch off Trueman to get rid of Mankad and then enjoying a handy spell with the ball. Making good use of the slope from the pavilion end, he was dipping the ball into the batsmen's pads, first bowling Phadkar then trapping Adhikari lbw. Allan was in the groove as seldom before in Test cricket. He later returned to have Shinde stumped by Evans, but his final figures of three for 37 might have been much better.

"I was two for 14 bowling with the slope and Len Hutton took me off. Alec Bedser couldn't believe it. He came across and said 'What the hell's he doing now?' And, when he brought me back, he put me on the wrong flaming end."

Hutton, Allan always felt, never really appreciated his qualities. He had passed disdainful comment on his century in Johannesburg three years earlier and now, just when Allan had felt he deserved an extended spell, Hutton had removed him from the attack. "I've got nothing to thank Len Hutton for," he says ruefully.

Brought up with the most colourful of county skippers, Allan found Hutton a dull captain. "All the amateurs had life in them. There was no life in Len Hutton. He just stood there and he said this and he said that, but there was no smile on his face. There was no personality to him. I didn't like hard men. I liked joyful men, people that skippered you with a laugh. I mean Wilf was a terror, but at certain times of a game he could smile, he could laugh and he'd even come out with a joke."

Allan was in fine form with the bat in the county game. Nine innings before the third Test at Old Trafford brought him five half-centuries with two scores over 90. But when the Test came he could manage only 4. With Trueman taking eight for 31, figures that would remain his best in Test cricket, India were dismissed for 58. Following on they made 82. Such dominance gave Allan no chance of a second innings, and as England's third seamer he was redundant, bowling just four overs.

Though his best seasons for Glamorgan lay ahead, Allan had played his last Test match. His place at The Oval went to Willie Watson, a specialist batsman, and when the Australians arrived in 1953 Trevor Bailey recovered the place he had lost early in 1951. His back-to-the-wall batting at Lord's and his uncompromising leg-side bowling to snuff out the Australians' victory quest at

Leeds kept England's Ashes hopes alive going into the Oval Test, where the urn finally changed hands. By this time Bailey was something of a cult hero and he became a fixture in the England side for the next five years, usually as the side's all-rounder and third seamer, though sometimes opening the bowling.

Only once, in the second Test of 1949, did Allan and Trevor Bailey play in the same England side. Though on the initial list of 19 whose availability was sounded out for the tour of the West Indies, Allan felt that, with Hutton as skipper, his chances of making the side were slim. Yet his stature in the English first-class game was still growing, and comparison of the two all-rounders suggests that, Allan, the older by nearly two years, was statistically the more valuable cricketer at this time.

	Watkins				Bailey		
	Runs	Ave	Wkt	Ave	Runs	Ave	Wkt	Ave
1952	1,267	32.48	88	21.47	1,513	36.90	103	29.09
1953	1,104	39.42	53	23.86	1,278	38.72	86	26.47
1954	1,640	34.89	103	15.82	1,344	32.78	101	21.39
1955	1,160	24.16	114	20.49	1,429	37.60	89	23.92

With an average of over 40 in Tests, there is a tendency to look upon Allan primarily as a batsman, while Bailey's stronger suit may have been bowling. Yet, for four consecutive years, Allan's bowling average in English first-class cricket was superior. Over this period he took 358 wickets at 19.89 against Bailey's 379 at 25.25. In two of those seasons he had a higher batting average and, while Bailey was a good fielder, it was Allan who had the reputation as a world-class catcher.

Injury cut down Allan's appearances in the summer of 1953, but that winter there was some compensation for missing the tour to the West Indies when he was asked to fly out to India to reinforce a Commonwealth team touring under the captaincy of the former Australian wicket-keeper Ben Barnett. Frank Worrell and Sonny Ramadhin had been called home to play for West Indies against England, and Allan and the Australian mystery bowler Jack Iverson joined the party as replacements.

Initially, Glamorgan had not been keen for Allan to take part in a full tour, but acceded to a later plea from manager George Duckworth, so on Christmas Eve he received his jabs prior to departing on Boxing Day. The Commonwealth team was not as strong as those that had toured earlier, winning only one of the five unofficial 'Tests'. For Allan, though, his seven matches

Commonwealth skipper Ben Barnett taking the field with Allan.

brought 357 runs at an average of 51, a prelude to an outstanding summer in 1954, a summer which would bring him a place for the first and only time in *Playfair's* eleven cricketers of the year.

In that miserably wet season, for the fourth year in a row, he topped his county's batting averages. His 1,640 runs were the most he had made in an English summer, and his 170 not out against Leicestershire at Swansea was to remain the highest score of his career. For the first time he completed the double, his 103 wickets coming at 15.82 each. On seven occasions he captured five wickets in an innings, crowning his season with seven for 28 in the final match against Derbyshire at Chesterfield, the best analysis of his career, in which, at one stage, he took four wickets in five balls. There were 29 first-class catches to complete his contribution to Glamorgan's rise to fourth place in the Championship, their best since 1948.

Chosen to play for MCC against the Pakistanis in May, Allan was still in the selectors' thoughts. Although he had not been on the list of those sounded out for availability to tour Australia, it seemed that his good form had brought him a place in the party when an extra man was to be chosen as a precaution against possible problems with Denis Compton's knee. "We were at Birmingham and Wilf said, 'Champagne's on you, Watty. You're going to Australia!'" Who passed this information to Wooller? And why was it wrong? Charles Palmer, until his death in 2005 the last survivor of those who picked the touring party, had no recollection of any committee discussion about this final place, and it seems that Hutton's preference for another left-hander, Vic Wilson from his own county, carried the day.

Like Allan, Wilson was a good close fielder, badly needed by a team from which both Trueman and Lock had been excluded. He had had a good season with the bat, but questions were asked about his technique for Australian pitches and he had no pretence to being a bowler. There were inspired selections for the tour, notably Frank Tyson and Colin Cowdrey, but Wilson was not one of them. Had Allan travelled, he might have replaced an under-used support bowler – by the end of the third Test, Wardle had bowled only 11 overs – and added welcome ballast to a batting order with a long tail. But it was not to be.

This was the man who had been one of the most surprising Test selections when pitted against Don Bradman's Invincibles. But six years later, when the selectors chose to overlook his claims, he was a far better cricketer. Peter Walker, who came into the Glamorgan side as Allan's powers were on the wane, remembers him as a brave batsman. "There were a lot of quick bowlers around then, but he never took a step towards square leg." A back-foot player, he was a strong hooker and cutter of the ball. "Anything short of a length, he was onto it straightaway," Don Shepherd says, "and he hit it flat, so it was a reasonably safe shot." Peter Walker echoes the views of others in recalling Allan as "a phenomenal player of wrist spin. George Tribe used to run through the rest of the world, but Allan always got runs against him."

Allan himself admits to being happier against wrist spin than conventional finger spinners. His method of playing wrist spinners never relied on watching the ball out of the hand. "As a back-foot player, I watched the ball in the air and I watched it off the wicket, and if it was up to me I just played it quietly back, but anything short or anything just outside my leg stick or even on the leg stick I used to sweep." He recalls battles won against the best wrist spinners of his time. "Eric Hollies wouldn't bowl leg spin at me; he bowled off spinners. Bruce Dooland didn't want to bowl when I came in to bat, and Jack Walsh once said to me at Swansea, 'For Christ's sake, Allan, stay at this end and let me have a go at Emrys!'"

Confronted by off spinners, turning the ball away from the left-hander, Allan resorted to the method advocated by Maurice Leyland when he had shared his batting secrets with the 17-year-old ground staff lad. He recalls playing Jim Laker at Swansea: "Right arm off spinner, leg breaks to me, I wouldn't drive him. I just played him quietly and, when he dropped the ball on the leg stick, I swept it. I'd got about three fours down there and Arthur McIntyre said to me, 'Allan, you do that once more and he'll be off.' So I swept him once more and he grabbed his cap and walked down to the sea end and that was the end of him. He took himself off!"

Allan sweeping.
The wicket-keeper is Surrey's Arthur McIntyre.

As a bowler, Allan could take the new ball and then come back with his Toshack-style cutters over the wicket. His slower method developed in the later stages of his career. It never involved extravagant spin, but he was a master of control and he could move the ball enough off the English pitches of his time to pitch on leg and cut past the off stump. "My memory is of him beating the bat so many times," says Don Shepherd, who reckons that bowlers who move the ball away from the bat are often unlucky.

Allan talks of the batsmen he has seen on television and their techniques – Gooch and Atherton shuffling in the crease. "I'd enjoy myself there," he says, and he agrees that his brain was always engaged whenever he bowled: "I never stopped thinking. I used to try to think what the batsman would want to do to me. And I had one thing in mind – to bowl it straight."

The complete all-rounder, Allan will be remembered above all for his close to the wicket fielding. Peter Walker, destined eventually to outstrip his 461 first-class catches, recalls how much he still had to learn when he first stood alongside his mentor. "It didn't

The Glamorgan leg trap.
Allan is at backward short leg with Phil Clift square
and Wilf Wooller at silly mid on.
The bowler is Jim McConnon.

matter what speed the ball came at him. Even when he was bowling and it was smashed back at him, it sort of melted into his hands. That was the thing that caught my eye about him, his ability to decelerate the pace off the ball in the matter of six inches or a foot. It stuck in my mind – how on earth did he do that?"

In Peter Walker's first match for Glamorgan, against Leicestershire at Llanelli, he stood alongside Allan in the field. Paradoxically they were in the slips, where Allan was never as happy as round the corner at leg slip where he could stretch out to catch the ball. It was also a first championship match for pace bowler Frank Clarke, who ran in to bowl before his young slip was ready. Leicestershire opener Gerry Lester flashed at the ball and Peter admits to hardly having seen it before Allan had dived and pouched it. "I was still trying to say, 'Where do I stand? Am I in the right place?' Allan just got up and carried on giving me advice, pausing only to catch this rocket projectile."

Allan made a close study of the art of catching. Despite his short fingers, he was blessed with safe hands, but he always preferred to have the ball coming to his left and positioned himself accordingly. He also liked to follow the flight of the ball from the bowler's hand, where others were schooled to watch the edge of the bat. Over the years at Glamorgan his waiting hands were fed by a succession of in-swing bowlers and some of the finest off spinners in the land, the sharp-spinning Johnnie Clay, the accurate Len Muncer, the flighty Jim McConnon and the one he found the hardest of all, Don Shepherd with his extra pace.

The demise of leg slips in the modern game is a puzzle to Allan. "They don't seem to worry about the ball flying down past the legs. The number of times in the day that they play that shot! It doesn't matter if he doesn't take a catch. With a leg slip, what it does – it stops the batsmen from playing the shot."

Chapter Nine
Problems in Pakistan

In 1955 Allan completed the double for a second time. Though his batting fell away, his 114 wickets were the most he had taken in a season. That winter he was selected, together with Maurice Tompkin of Leicestershire and Somerset wicket-keeper Harold Stephenson, as one of three older professionals, to provide experience on an MCC A tour of Pakistan. Led by his old friend Donald Carr, the party set off expecting to play most of their matches on turf. "We'd been told that, of the 14 or 15 matches we were going to play, 11 would be on turf and four on matting," says Donald Carr. "When we got there we found it was the other way round. And Fazal Mahmood was the greatest matting wicket bowler there's ever been, I would think."

It was always going to be a tough tour. Since Allan's last visit four years earlier, the host country had won Test status and shared a series in England, so they were not best pleased to receive a side in which only Tony Lock could claim to be a regular Test player. The matches were marred by poor umpiring. Was it incompetence or bias? Donald Carr's view is quite clear: "Well, I think I can say that all members of my team considered it was biased."

On top of these problems was a feud that developed between the two captains. "A.H.Kardar," Allan mutters disdainfully. "Donald did warn me. He was so anti-British it was nobody's business. That didn't make for good comradeship on the tour." Kardar had been in the same Oxford side as Carr and, although the Pakistani had been "a bit of an odd cove", Donald had found him perfectly friendly. "I had expected a friendly series," he says.

The trouble started with a speech by the MCC captain at a dinner after the second match of the tour, against the Governor General's XI in Karachi. Donald Carr had earlier been asked whether Kardar had had a nickname when he was at Oxford. He had replied that he was sometimes known as 'the mystic of the East'. The inquisitor had misunderstood Carr's answer and it went the rounds that

Hafeez Kardar was 'the mistake of the East'. The captain chose to make jocular reference to this in his speech. "It went down very well at this dinner, I thought."

It was only later in the tour, when they had reached Lahore for the first representative match, that Donald Carr came to feel that his speech had been an error of judgement. The two teams were staying in the same hotel, where Carr was having dinner with other team members when Kardar walked in. "I was near the door and I said, 'Hello, Hafeez' and he ignored me and went on his way with his pals." Wondering what was up, Carr finished his meal and went over to the table where the Pakistan captain was sitting with his friends. "I said, 'Hello, Hafeez, nice to see you.' He just said, 'Hello', only just, and carried on talking to his friends."

The frostiness persisted until the time for the toss. "As we started walking out, he said, 'Donald, that speech you made in Karachi, it was the most disgraceful thing I've ever heard.' I'd forgotten all about it. I said that we'd been friends at Oxford. He just said, 'It was disgusting.' So I said, 'Sorry about it but, if you can't take it, we'd better go and toss up.' That's what started the troubles that ended up with the umpire having water thrown at him a few matches later."

Between the ructions off the field, thanks principally to Tony Lock, whose 81 wickets came at 10.61 each, MCC won seven of their 14 first-class matches, though losing the four-match representative series by two to one. For most of the batsmen it was a disappointing tour, only Peter Richardson seriously enhancing his reputation. Allan had a lean time with the bat and took only seven wickets. He was now used less as a stock bowler and had to take the new ball in several matches after Mike Cowan had been forced to return home with back trouble, leaving Alan Moss as the only other pace bowler until Ian Thomson of Sussex arrived as a reinforcement.

The Lahore match saw Pakistan's batsmen at their most tedious. Having dismissed MCC for 204, the home side took 210 overs to make 363 for nine in reply, Hanif Mohammad occupying the crease for eight and three-quarter hours to reach his hundred. This funereal pace allowed the tourists to escape with a draw.

MCC had been disenchanted with several umpiring decisions and, as they were entitled to do, they lodged an objection to one of the officials, Idris Begh. As they moved on to their next representative match at Dacca in East Pakistan, the modern Bangladesh, they had confidently expected to find a replacement. But when they arrived, who should be there but Begh? "I asked him, 'What are you doing here?'" says Donald Carr. "He said, 'I'm here for the tiger season.' Anyway, he turned out on the field of play on the first day. And he rather obviously gave us the advantage in a number of appeals."

Help from one of the umpires – there was certainly none from the other – proved in vain as Khan Mohammad and Fazal Mahmood, relishing the matting pitch, took all twenty MCC wickets. The absence of Cowan, in conditions that were tailor-made for a bowler of his pace, was a severe blow to MCC, who lost by an innings and ten runs.

It was off the field at Dacca that developments for which the tour is immortalised first began to take shape. A party of high-spirited young men found themselves closeted in a then relatively poor country, predominantly Moslem, still recovering from the problems of Partition. Where there had been an excess of social and civic occasions when Allan toured India, now there were too many evenings with nothing much to do. Water pistols were one of

MCC A team in Pakistan.
Back row (l to r): Mohammad Sharif, Fred Titmus, Brian Close, Ian Thomson, Roy Swetman, Jim Parks, Peter Sainsbury, Peter Richardson, Ken Barrington, M.Azghar.
Front row: Maurice Tompkin, M.H.Khawaja, Zafar Ullah, Tony Lock, Azmal Ullah, Bill Sutcliffe (vice capt), C.G.Howard (Manager), Allan Watkins, Daud Khan (Liaison officer).
The MCC captain Donald Carr is absent.

the answers to the players' boredom, and the practice of administering a fuller dousing found a ready target in the form of George Duckworth. "George was working for the British Council or something," Donald Carr recalls, "and he had to receive the water treatment. It was in the room of one of the players and Idris, with a friend of his, walked past the door of that room. I chased after him. I thought he can make trouble out of our pouring water over George Duckworth. But he was laughing about it, so I said, 'It's all right, we'll get you before the end of the tour.' He chuckled away and said, 'Oh no, you'll never catch me.' And we did catch him at Peshawar!"

After the disappointment of Dacca, there were innings victories against a Combined XI and Punjab as the party moved on towards the Khyber Pass and the ancient city of Peshawar. Allan was omitted from the side for this third representative match, which once again saw two wretched batting displays from the tourists and a second victory for Pakistan, this time by seven wickets. Off the field MCC had greater 'success', managing to capture Idris Begh for his ritual ducking.

"It would have been perfectly all right," Donald Carr maintains, "except that, after he'd had the water treatment, two of the Pakistani players walked into our room – they were staying in a different hotel, but they'd come up – and, when they saw Idris in a rather bedraggled state, they roared with laughter. This was too much for Idris, to be laughed at by his own folk. He suddenly disappeared out of the room and had taken himself off to Hafeez Kardar in their hotel, where it is rumoured he was sharing a room with Hafeez – I'm not sure if he was. And that was real trouble time, which was sad."

Seven or eight of the team had been involved in administering the ducking, but Allan was not one of them. "I came back and I heard a hell of a noise, and I said, 'What the hell's going on?' They said, 'We've had the water treatment for the umpire.' He'd taken it in good part until the members of the Pakistani team had come in and laughed. That put the kibosh on it."

The diplomacy of manager Geoffrey Howard averted an even greater fuss as MCC sent cables from London offering to terminate the tour. At a subsequent enquiry back in England, Donald Carr would accept responsibility for what had been a misplaced prank bereft of malice.

A two-wicket win in the final representative match at Karachi provided some compensation for what had been the least satisfactory of Allan's three tours in MCC colours. His own form had been poor and, in contrast to the gentle Indians, whom he had enjoyed playing against, he had now found a more belligerent attitude on the pitch.

Off the field there had been little entertainment. "It was a dull tour, nothing for the boys to do, nothing planned for them." Allan had enjoyed Carr's leadership, and there had always been a good spirit running through the team. He had shared a room with Maurice Tompkin, who was to die tragically young only months later. "What a wonderful man. He was a handsome looking bloke. All the girls on the boat went for him." Another good mate was the vice-captain, Billy Sutcliffe. "He was always looking for me to go and have a pint of beer with him. Nobody else seemed to drink."

With so little to do, the team were for ever kicking footballs about and on more than one occasion they were persuaded to play a competitive match. Both Allan and Donald Carr talk animatedly of the day they beat "a team which was in the semi-final of the Pakistan Cup or something". They won by two goals to nil that day in Multan, when an early conclusion to their match with the Railways XI meant finding another way to entertain the spectators. As news of a football match spread, the crowd multiplied and around 20,000 were there to watch.

"We said we'd only play if we played in pumps," Allan remembers. This was the only concession. The pitch was marked out properly and posts were put up on the cricket field. Several of the touring party had experience of league football. The captain, himself a member of Pegasus teams that reached the FA Amateur Cup Final, pinpoints the strength of the side: "Watkins at left half, Closey at centre half, who knocked everyone over, and Stephenson at right half – they were the backbone of the team." Ken Barrington kept goal, the Sussex pair of Parks and Thomson were at back, and the forward line read Lock, Tompkin, Swetman, Carr and Titmus. The only weakness, the captain felt, was Lock. "I'm not quite sure why he was playing. I think he fixed up the game."

A large silver cup was on display before the game started and many dignitaries from Pakistan football paraded in the stand. "But at the end of the game," says Donald Carr, "they'd all disappeared, just as I was preparing to lead the team up to get this cup."

As the memories fade, there is one that Allan will not easily forget: a night when they had visited Calcutta on their way back from East Pakistan. "We stayed at an old colonel's place. I'd had a few drinks, of course, and when I got to bed I forgot to put the old mosquito net over me. I got bitten all over the place."

Chapter Ten
The Strain Becomes Too Much

On Allan's return to England Molly noticed that there was still evidence of the mosquito bites all over his body. He felt under the weather, apparently nursing a cold, and retired to bed. Molly sent for the doctor, a friend of the family for whom she worked. "He said, 'What's the matter, Allan?' I said, 'I don't know. I'm perspiring. I'm a bit weak.' He said, 'Let's have a look at you.' He pulled back the sheet. 'Oh God, Molly, he's got malaria. Can't you smell it?'"

It had taken some weeks for the illness to develop, but for many years to come, Allan would feel the effects. He was able to take his place in the county side as usual when the 1956 season started, but it soon became clear that he was not the player he had been. "I hadn't the same energy for a while. I think I'd had enough cricket, too." Though *Wisden* still thought his efforts this season 'untiring', for the first time since he had established himself in the Glamorgan side, Allan failed to reach his thousand runs, and his bag of wickets fell to 58, barely half the number he had captured the previous summer. He would remain a key member of the county team for another four years and his form would recover, but his best cricketing days were over.

There had been three operations on his cartilages and he was beginning to pay the price for the years of whole-hearted effort as an all-rounder. Molly's words from when I had first called at the Watkins' home came back: "I used to say, 'I wish you had a job like Gilbert Parkhouse, standing there with his arms folded.'" The stylish opening batsman with a taste for Beaujolais had concerned himself only with batting. There was no bowling and, as a regular first slip, not much running around in the field. Nor had Parkhouse often wasted energy on debating the team's tactics. But Allan was involved in every aspect of the game, and nothing was done in half measures. Passing his opinion on a Test cricketer from another county, Allan once pointed to his heart and then to his stomach.

"That's what he always lacked," was his verdict. "No heart and no guts." No-one would ever have said this of Allan.

He was starting to become a regular on the masseur's table. Lunchtimes after fielding meant a trip to see John Evans, Glamorgan's long-serving physio. "It was, 'Pint of shandy for Allan in the masseur's room.' Then John would say, 'Right take your trousers down,' and he would massage my legs with ether to keep them going." It was the regular massaging, Allan reckons, that helped to extend his playing career into the 1960s.

All the time, unsuspected by the crowd watching the commitment of the feisty bulldog figure on the field, Allan was wracked by nervous tension. "I underestimated my own abilities," he now feels, "and I had to make up for it by hard work. And there were these nerves." He was always nervous waiting to bat, and it was the same when he first went on to bowl. "I always used to hope and pray that the first ball was a good one. But Haydn Davies was most peculiar. He used to say, 'I hope they hit him for a four in the first over. Because they won't get another one out of him after that for four or five overs.'" Perhaps perversely, aggression from the batsman helped to settle Allan's nerves and stiffened his resolve. The key to it all was getting involved, so fielding wasn't a problem. "I was quite happy at short leg. I enjoyed that. I dropped a few, of course, but I don't think I dropped too many."

It had been the same in his days as a soccer player. "I would sit in the dressing room and the perspiration would fall off my chin. The Scottish coach we had used to say, 'For Christ's sake, Allan, stop it. You've been going for 45 minutes of football already.' The back of my shirt would be wet with perspiration. Just nerves, and yet as soon as I got on the field and ran around, I couldn't care less."

In the Glamorgan side of the 1950s Jim McConnon was notorious for a lack of self-belief when the chips were down, and it was Willie Jones, always in fear of his captain, who was said to be the one most wracked by nerves, but Don Shepherd believes Allan suffered more: "Willie could talk about it and have a few pints, but Allan bottled it up."

After the disappointment of 1956, Allan's batting average for the next three years crept back over 30, never a bad figure on Welsh pitches, but the changing shape of the team meant that fewer demands were made of his bowling. Don Shepherd had now converted from pace merchant to medium-paced off spinner. A man who never wanted to surrender the ball, Shepherd became the bowler to whom successive captains would turn for more than a decade to maintain control. Meanwhile Peter Walker was gradually taking over Allan's role as the left-armer in the attack. By 1959 he was sending down more than twice the overs of Allan.

The late 1950s were not easy times for Glamorgan, and problems came to a head in 1958. With his 46th birthday approaching, Wilf Wooller expressed a wish to retire. As captain-cum-secretary many felt he enjoyed too much power, and a wrangle over whether he should be allowed to retain his position as secretary without a cut in salary split the county's complex governing body. A powerful faction wanted him out of the club altogether, and there were mass resignations before a referendum ended in Wooller's favour.

The question of who should succeed the man who had captained the county since 1947 soon set the conspirators to work. Though Haydn Davies was still senior professional, he had been dropped as wicket-keeper in favour of David Evans. Now 46, he was ready to retire, and Allan believes that he harboured no ambitions to lead. The idea of bringing in an outsider had support, and Allan remembers that there had been thoughts that Billy Sutcliffe, his old pal from the Pakistan tour, might be lured from Yorkshire, where he had been superseded as captain. "He was coming, but his dad wouldn't hear of it."

To muddy the waters there was a comical interlude when a corpulent 34-year-old science master from Eton College, Tolly Burnett, was drafted in to play in the last eight matches of the season. Burnett was the not wholly innocent pawn of some of the anti-Wooller plotters, and he was sprung with minimal formality on the Glamorgan dressing room. Here, it seemed, was the heir apparent, someone who might take a year or two on sabbatical to lead the county.

To seasoned professional cricketers it was a baffling, even insulting, move. "I don't know where they found him," Allan says. "How they could ever have thought of him taking over from Wilf! He had no idea of cricket. He batted like a 14-year-old. He stood right away from the bat. Where he'd played his cricket I don't know." It came as a surprise to Allan to be told that A.C.Burnett had won a Cambridge Blue in 1949. "Good God, well he didn't look a cricketer!" With Wooller away for the last two matches, Burnett's talent for leadership was cruelly exposed. The sidelining of Haydn

Davies meant that Allan was the skipper's right hand man. "I remember he wanted to put himself on to bowl," he says with incredulity. Seventy-one runs from 11 innings, some ponderous fielding and no obvious tactical insight or understanding of the first-class game's subtleties, spelt the end of any enthronement plans.

With all the plots and counter-plots off the field, it was hard for the players to keep focussed on their jobs, and the county slid to fifteenth in the table. One of the few whose form did not suffer was Allan. His wickets shot up from 26 to 77 and he now topped both batting and bowling averages.

Nothing was ever said officially, but Wooller had dropped hints to Allan that he was earmarked to be his successor. And the hints were not welcome. "I was worried that it was me going to be skipper, and I didn't want it." Allan's anxieties were assuaged when Wooller, having seen the back of those who had schemed for his downfall, reversed his decision to retire. His reinstatement could only be a short-term solution to the problems Glamorgan faced, but he continued as captain for two more years.

After the disharmony of the previous year, the long, hot summer of 1959 saw a revival in Glamorgan's fortunes. His authority restored, Wooller led the side with renewed zest and his players responded. Parkhouse had his best ever season, Hedges, McConnon and Shepherd all showed improved form, while Walker made a big advance as an all-rounder. From fifteenth, Glamorgan rose to sixth in the table, and were only denied second place when the last two Middlesex wickets eluded them in their final match.

With Haydn Davies retiring at the end of the 1958 season, Allan had become senior professional. For some counties with an inexperienced amateur in charge this was a crucial appointment, but it had never been so at Glamorgan, where the players knew that Wilf Wooller would always represent their interests to the committee and that they could rely on him to defend them to the outside world. "There was no need really of a senior professional with Wilf. If I heard a bit grumbling among the team, I used to say 'Come on, you know Wilf, you know his temperament. You know what will happen: tomorrow he'll be laughing and joking.' That's all I had to do. It was different on tour."

Since his appointment as a Test selector in 1955 Wooller had missed some county matches each season, and in 1959 he handed over to Allan, now aged 37, for eight championship matches. He enjoyed mixed fortunes, with three solid championship victories balanced by three defeats. Two of the losses were by emphatic margins to strong Yorkshire and Surrey sides, but the third, against Kent at Dartford, was a desperately close run affair with Allan's bold declaration enabling the home team to sneak home by one wicket in the last over of the match. "Allan, without you there wasn't a game," he remembers a Kent committee man saying. It had been wonderful cricket, but Allan knew he had lost, and it worried him.

For a man consumed by self doubt, Allan's next match in charge, against Warwickshire at Edgbaston, was equally disturbing. After Glamorgan's batsmen had fought their way back into the match, Shepherd and McConnon made victory look a formality, only for Basil Bridge and Ossie Wheatley, one of the game's undisputed rabbits, to resist all efforts to dislodge them in a partnership that lasted 45 minutes.

Allan also harbours mixed memories of an early season triumph when he had captained against the Indians. He had seen his bowlers take the last six wickets cheaply to secure a win by 51 runs, so it left a sour taste to hear his team's efforts belittled when Wilf Wooller went into the Indians' dressing room. "Bad luck chaps," he had said. "If you had won the toss you'd have won the game." Unknown to Wooller, Don Shepherd had been in the dressing room collecting autographs and heard his skipper's comments. "That was Wilf's congratulations to me for winning the ruddy game!" says Allan. "That's the sort of chap he was."

Had he been given the captaincy, Allan feels that he would have settled into the role, but he had uncomfortable memories of some of the occasions on which he had deputised. In 1960, his final season, Wooller missed eleven matches. Allan led against Kent in a drawn early season game at Cardiff, but thereafter he stepped down in favour of Gilbert Parkhouse, Don Shepherd taking charge for one match at Westcliff. There had been a bad mid-season trot, nine matches without a win, when Glamorgan travelled to Liverpool to play a strong Lancashire side with eyes on the Championship. Parkhouse was injured and Allan had been expected to take up the reins once more. But the demons returned as he lay in bed that night, reminding him of that narrow loss to Kent. "I woke up in the morning and I thought, 'I can't do it.' Something seemed to tell me that I couldn't be responsible. I couldn't get my mind together to concentrate on running things, taking the boys out. I just couldn't do it." Don Shepherd took over and Glamorgan won a famous victory in the dying moments of the game as storm clouds encircled the ground waiting only for Glamorgan to take the final wicket before swamping the whole area.

"I lived on my nerves all my life." Allan so often repeats these words. For some years he had been afflicted by asthma, and the tightness of his chest made it harder to get fit, but it had not stopped him competing. Now the debilitating effects of asthma were compounded by tension. It all came to a head at Swansea. "I was batting and I had these horrible pains in my chest. I gave my wicket away and I remember Wilf coming down the steps. He opened the door and was going to give me a rollicking. I was sat in the corner and he said, 'My God, what's wrong with you?' I said, 'I've got pains in my chest. I feel terrible.' He said, 'Right, straight to Morriston Hospital.'"

Allan's doctor later had a private word with Molly. "You know what your doctor has been saying," she said. "If you don't ease up, he won't be responsible for your health." Allan thought about his family. He knew Molly was right, but he did not retire immediately, and he was still the senior professional when the 1961 season opened with a new captain. Ossie Wheatley, a former Cambridge Blue, had been lured from Warwickshire as an opening bowler and skipper.

Wheatley speaks of inheriting a team in transition where Allan's experience as senior professional would have been invaluable. "He was a super guy, but he wasn't very well. He had asthma and he was very nervous." Allan played eight matches, but his captain found that, with his nerves, he always needed to work himself up to play. He had managed a couple of fifties, but injury forced him to drop out of the side at the beginning of June. A month later Glamorgan were at Lord's when his new captain tried to persuade Allan to play again. "I said, 'Come on, Allan, it would be nice to have you on the field, just as a batsman.' He said, 'I need a bit of time to think about that.' I said, 'Come on you've been playing for 20 years.' He said, 'No, no I really do need time.'" The worrying had finally got the better of Allan. In an era when many careers extended well into the forties, he was only 39, but he had played his last game for Glamorgan. "He was a great loss," Ossie Wheatley says with obvious sadness.

Cricket has never brought Allan great riches. When I had first met the Watkins, Molly had described the ritual of laundering his kit in the Bridge Inn flat. "Sometimes he used to get home at nine o'clock at night and he'd have to catch the nine o'clock bus in the morning, before we had a car, to get back to Cardiff. So I had to wash his clothes, dry them by the fire and iron them so he could take them back next morning. I didn't complain. It was the way it was done." One day it was Allan who complained, "I said, 'Darling, you've got the crease in the wrong place.' This was about 11 o'clock at night. The next thing I was ducking and the flat iron hit the wall!"

Playing representative cricket meant that Allan had been better rewarded than some, but it was his benefit in 1955, bringing in £5,000, that provided his only capital. Recognising the passion for cricket in the west of Wales, the nursery for so many of the county's best players, Allan forsook the chance of a match at Newport and chose the Gloucestershire match at Swansea for his benefit. Though he speaks not a word of Welsh, the Swansea supporters still took him to their heart as one of their own. His match was badly hit by the weather. With no play on the third day, receipts were only £280, but the county's followers rallied round to ensure that he received a nest egg worthy of his contribution to the Glamorgan cause.

Allan's first priority with his benefit money was to secure the best education he could afford for his four children, and by the time of his retirement from cricket both his sons were in private schools. Meanwhile he took the opportunity to buy a retail dairy business in the main street in Usk. By a strange coincidence, this was the very shop in which his mother had worked before the war, but now it was to provide an outlet for Molly's business skills. "She was very able mathematically," son Allen recalls, speaking in admiration of his mother's commercial acumen.

A forerunner of the modern delicatessen, the shop sold a wide range of groceries while specialising in cream, made at the back of the premises, and cheeses, which were stored in the cellars and cut to customers' requirements. Molly was soon extending the range of cheeses and hams, and when Christmas came there were fresh turkeys in the shop. Judith remembers how busy it became and all the family did their bit to help, with 'Auntie Eileen', Selwyn's wife, roped in to help. A delivery service was always available and young Allen remembers that, as soon as he passed his driving test, he was

The therapist's shop that was once a dairy.
The memorably named neighbour has also moved in
since the Watkins gave up their shop.

behind the wheel of the van delivering to customers in all the outlying villages. "The shop paid for our education," he says.

With living accommodation behind and above the shop, there was no further need for the house in Ladysmith. The shop became the family home and the children remember vast refrigerators that were always good for raiding for a tasty bacon snack. The shop's business has changed with the gentrification of Usk. Now it is home to a therapist who offers holistic massage, lifestyle management and body shaping. But in its heyday it provided a welcome bed for the night for players from Swansea and beyond when Glamorgan were playing in Cardiff. Don Shepherd, whose home was in the Gower peninsula, was one who often appreciated the Watkins' hospitality. He remembers well the times that he and Bernard Hedges slept over the shop, though the building's location on the main road through the town to Pontypool brought a few disturbed nights. "Lorries went thundering through and you could feel the whole area shaking."

As Allan contemplated retirement he did not have long to wait before a job presented itself, with an invitation to join the Borstal Service. An enterprising governor of the local open prison for boys wanted to broaden the horizons of his young charges, so Allan was appointed as a prison officer with special responsibility for sport. He tackled his new job with relish. He found that the boys were already playing darts, table tennis and billiards. Darts was one of the few games which Allan never mastered, but he was a proficient table tennis player and he had been introduced to billiards on Mr Rickards' table at Usk Priory. It was not long before Allan had got the boys playing badminton too, while he also directed his attention to outdoor sports. With the aid of a party of boys, he set about draining land for rugby and soccer. Then he moved on to cricket, once again getting the boys involved in laying a pitch. "Eventually we got it so good that the deputy governor said, 'I'm playing in the next match on there.'"

Allan encouraged the boys in competition, and he had particular fun with table tennis. "The boys loved me because they'd have a smart guy come into the prison and he might have been a good table tennis player, and he'd come in and have a knock with the others first. They'd say, 'We've got a smart guy on the table, sir, come and show him something will you?' So I would go up the alleyway and watch this boy play. I was left-handed and I was quite useful at table tennis, so I would watch him. Then I'd say, 'Come on. I'll give you a game.' Touch wood I never lost, but I only ever played the one game. I would never give him another chance. I'd watch him, but he never knew my game."

Allan's role in the prison meant that he enjoyed a special rapport with the governor. He was allowed to take the boys out in the evenings for badminton matches and, when the top brass came down from London, the former Test cricketer would find himself the centre of interest. "All the others were stood to attention and when they came to me they were shaking my hand." Allan felt awkward about this special treatment. "It didn't go down too well," he reflects. For one superior officer it was too much. Determined to bring Allan down to earth, he made a point of constantly picking on him for the slightest irregularity.

One night Allan was a few minutes late locking up and returning the keys. "This fellow started blasting me. I said, 'You're always after me, so I'm finished.' And he laughed in my face. He said, 'I've heard all this before.'" Next morning Allan went to see the governor and resigned. Molly had encouraged Allan to stick to his guns in making this decision. She was finding life in the shop hard work on top of her duties as a wife and mother, and she had seen a change in her husband brought on by the stress of his work. "They are a certain breed, prison officers, and she said I was coming into the house and barking my orders. 'Do this.' 'Do that.' And she wasn't liking it. I didn't know I was doing it."

Molly knew what was best for Allan. "Go back to what you love." she said. "Go and get yourself a job coaching."

Chapter Eleven
'Go Back to What You Love'

If he was to move into coaching, Allan's first thought was to get in touch with his old friend Donald Carr, who had retired from playing and was now an assistant secretary with MCC. Carr's advice was that he should go up to Lord's for a full coaching course. This went against the grain for Allan: "I'd heard all the tales about Lord's – how you mustn't do this, you mustn't do that. You must hold it this way and you're holding it that way." To Allan it all sounded so negative, and he knew that the coaches at Lord's would never have countenanced the grip that he had inherited from Maurice Leyland. He turned down Donald Carr's advice, but was nevertheless pleased to learn of possible coaching opportunities.

The rest of Allan's working life would be devoted to coaching at English public schools. His only qualification was a career stretching over 20 years as a professional cricketer, but it had taught him all he needed to know, and to this he brought his own philosophy of taking a positive view of a young cricketer's natural inclinations. "Some of the people you coach, they've got shots and they may look awful, but it's their strong point, so you develop it. And that's what I've tried to do all my life."

Allan was engaged to do some pre-season coaching at Christ College, Brecon. Then, in 1964, he obtained a full-time position at Framlingham College, a public school a few miles inland from the Suffolk coast. It took courage to uproot himself, his son David feels. Though cricket had made him a member of the wider South Wales community, Allan's home had always been in Usk and this was where he belonged. The move to East Anglia provided him with a qualification to play for Suffolk in the Minor Counties Championship. The suggestion that he might do so came about when he became friendly with Cyril Perkins, one of the legendary figures of the Minor Counties game, whose left-arm spinners brought him 779 wickets for Suffolk. Perkins was coach at Ipswich School, one of Framlingham's opponents, and he persuaded Allan to make himself available for the Suffolk team.

Turning out in seven matches in 1965 and 1966, he made a steady if unspectacular contribution. With the bat he averaged 25.30, with one fifty against Buckinghamshire, and he took 19 wickets at 18.47. A highlight of Allan's Suffolk career was helping his side to qualify for a place in the Gillette Cup. He recalls the tensions of the match against Nottinghamshire Second XI that secured Suffolk a home tie against Kent. But, when their big match came round, Allan opted not to play. "I said, 'I'm not playing. You let the young boys enjoy their pleasure of playing against Colin Cowdrey and all of them. I've done it for so many years. It would make no difference to me.' So I didn't play."

Allan and Molly settled happily into life at Framlingham. The coaching was soon going well for Allan, while Molly found a job with a greengrocer in the town. There she soon made an impression on the shop's owner by suggesting that they should offer fruit and vegetables at reduced prices to the older customers instead of throwing them out. "She more or less doubled the takings," Allan says. They were both content with their lot, when, in 1970, a new opportunity presented itself: Arnold Dyson was about to retire at Oundle.

A larger and more famous public school near Peterborough in Northants, its foundation dating back to 1556, Oundle's links with Glamorgan had begun fortuitously back in 1946 when the Welshmen were playing Warwickshire at Edgbaston. In the home team was Michael Mills, a Cambridge blue that year and destined to captain the University in 1948. He recalls being approached by Austin Matthews, who had coached at Stowe School before the war but was now playing a full season for Glamorgan. Matthews told Mills that Arnold Dyson would soon be retiring from county cricket and that he was looking for a position with a public school. An Old Oundelian, Mills had a word in the appropriate ear and Dyson's long career at the school started in 1948.

Oundle's strong cricket tradition in post-war years owes much to Michael Mills, who returned to his old school to devote his whole working life to teaching there. He ran the cricket for many years and was immediately elected secretary and treasurer of the Oundle Rovers, the old boys' side. At the age of 85, more than 20 years after retiring from teaching, he was still looking after the Rovers in 2006, when a dinner held in London that autumn, with Allan in attendance, celebrated his devotion to the cause.

In the late 1960s, when Arnold Dyson was due to retire, Michael Mills recalls the bursar's gloomy prediction. "You'll never replace a character like Arnold Dyson," he said. "We can if we try," Mills replied. A letter was sent to all the county secretaries. By this time the Glamorgan link had been strengthened through Wilfred Wooller sending his two sons to Oundle, where they were in Mills' house, and it was from Wooller that the most helpful reply came. "Try Allan Watkins," he suggested. Allan travelled to Oundle for an interview. "Mike, you are quite right," the bursar said later. Oundle had found a worthy successor to Dyson. "He was an absolute gem," says Mills, "and of course he was playing in that game when Austin Matthews had spoken to me!"

Allan could see that a move to Oundle would be a promotion and bring a better salary. The Framlingham bursar acquiesced, to the disgust of Norman Borrett, the master in charge of cricket. A useful cricketer for Devon, who had made three appearances for Essex, Borrett was more renowned as a hockey international and had a legendary reputation for his ruthlessness on a squash court, where he had been British amateur champion. A born competitor, he was determined that Allan was not going to leave without a fight. "He came up to the house and got hold of his cheque book and opened it. He said, 'There you are, Allan, sign and put your wages on there. What the school can't pay, the old boys will make up.'"

There had been other compensations at Framlingham, where Allan was regarded as a member of the Common Room. This gave him a schoolmaster's pension rights, whereas at Oundle he would not be treated as one of the teaching staff, so his pension would suffer. Nevertheless Allan was impressed by the facilities he saw at Oundle and by the eagerness of the school to hire him.

Oundle's cricketing traditions had been reinforced in 1968 with the appointment of Dr Barry Trapnell as headmaster. A good enough cricketer to have won a blue at Cambridge and opened the bowling for the Gentlemen against the Players in 1946, Trapnell had toyed with a longer involvement in the game but, after one match for Middlesex, the captain of the day, R.W.V.Robins, made clear the commitment he expected. Sadly, this clashed with Trapnell's academic and other aspirations. "One day," he recalls, "I received a message from Robins saying that he wished me to play against the Indians. 'Sorry,' I replied 'I'll be climbing mountains with my chemistry master.'"

Dr Trapnell came to Oundle at a time of great change for the traditional public schools. It was an immense challenge. "Everything had to be rethought out," he says. His other priorities precluded much direct involvement with cricket, but he remembers Allan as "a very dear man, much respected and loved." Later on, when Trapnell was succeeded by David McMurray, a Free Forester who lists cricket as the first of his recreations, Allan found that he could always rely on the headmaster's support and, when the time came for him to retire on his 65th birthday, it was McMurray who persuaded him to carry on coaching for another five years.

Cricket at Oundle

Michael Mills forged a formidable partnership with Allan, as did his successor as cricket master, Jeremy Firth. "Chaps loved sitting around in the dressing room talking to him," Mills says. "He was a terrific talker and a very good coach." Oundle still awaits its first Test cricketer, but the fruits of Allan's coaching were seen in the successes of the Oundle Rovers in the Cricketer Cup, the knockout competition for old boys' sides from the leading public schools. Twice runners-up in the 1970s, those who had passed through Allan's hands won the cup three times in five years from 1985.

The nucleus of the successful Rovers side came together in the school teams of the mid-1970s, when Peter Mills, Michael's son, was one of those involved. He particularly recalls the 1976 team, four of whom went on to win blues: John Knight at Oxford, David Holliday, Ian Hodgson and Peter himself at Cambridge, where he led the 1982 side against Oxford when Derek Pringle preferred to play for England in a Test match, thereby enabling the Mills to provide the only instance of a father and son captaining the Light Blues. Michael Mills travelled up for the match, taking the school coach with him. "I was so proud," Allan says. "It was something to have one of our boys playing, and we had three in the one team one year. It was a great occasion."

Peter Mills talks with great enthusiasm of the way they played their matches at Oundle and gives unstinting credit to Allan. "He said the right amount technically without ever trying to say too much.

*Allan returns to Usk with Tony Lewis and Jeff Jones
for the testimonial of Phil Clift (foreground)*

He made the game simple, and his culture was that it was a game to be to be enjoyed, and a team game. And he always taught us to play positively." Around this time first-class cricket was starting to see time-honoured standards of sportsmanship slipping. This was anathema to Allan and it strengthened his resolve in coaching his teams. "He had no time for gamesmanship," Peter Mills says. "Allan was a true sportsman. He would not encounter disrespect to the opposition."

Allan's enthusiasm – all his chat on a Friday evening before a match, his stories of touring with the likes of Denis Compton – rubbed off on the players. Peter Mills feels sure that this was why those who had played together in the 1970s were so keen to return each year to play for the Rovers. And when they came back to Oundle, they would find Molly and Peter's own mother doing the catering for their matches. "They were a unit, Allan and Molly," Peter says, remembering how Molly ran the school sports shop. As in the dairy at Usk, she was the business brains, but Allan loved being in the shop for the chance of a natter.

The privileged world of a public school contrasted sharply with the struggles of Allan's own childhood. His family and those around them at Usk had always been solid Labour supporters. "It went through family after family. Wilf and I used to have bloody good arguments about Conservatives and Labour. His father was only a garage owner in North Wales, but he was lucky enough to get a good education. I used to pull his leg about the bus going up another penny and all this sort of thing."

In his playing days, Allan had resented the good fortune of those born to an easier, more leisurely life. He had questioned the credentials of some of those perhaps too hastily recognised for their deeds on the cricket fields of Oxford or Cambridge, but he has mellowed with the passage of time. "When I came into the system I realised that they were lads the same as anybody else. They were decent chaps, but it's a different world."

Now Allan can look back on pleasures shared with the boys, and he particularly relishes an occasion when he was the privileged one. The Oundle cricket team had gone on tour to Guernsey and made a trip to visit Alderney. Their minibus paused. "This is John Arlott's house," said their guide. This was Allan's cue. "I said, 'I know John Arlott very well. I wonder how he is.' And one of the smart arses said, 'Well go in and find out.' So I said, 'All right, I will go in and find out.' They didn't quite believe me, but I went and knocked and a lady came to the door and I said, 'Is Mr John Arlott at home?' She said, 'I don't know. Who are you?' I said, 'I'm Allan Watkins.' She said, 'Oh, Allan, come in.' This was John's second wife. In the kitchen John opened two bottles of wine. He had the red and I had the white. There we were drinking and a knock came on the door. John's wife went to the door and I could hear voices. 'Is Mr Watkins coming or staying?' She said, 'Mr Watkins is with John in the kitchen and he's staying!'" Later that day, when Allan had re-joined the boys, he was presented with a bottle of port. "Here you are, Allan, we won't disbelieve you again!"

When his coaching days were over and they had to give up the home provided by the school, Allan and Molly thought about returning to Usk; but they decided to stay in Oundle, moving into another house in the same residential area of the town. Allan now had the chance to play more golf and he and Molly enjoyed holidays abroad, with Malta a particularly favoured retreat. Their retirement was the more contented for knowing that all four of their children had found good jobs.

Both sons, now retired, rose to hold important positions in the teaching profession and each of them had moments when they threatened to emulate their father's sporting eminence. Both boys excelled at rugby. Allen played for Pontypool, where he stood in for Clive Rowlands, when the Welsh scrum half was on international duty. After moving to Suffolk, he played divisional rugby for Eastern Counties and, had he not moved to the Midlands, Allan believes he might have challenged for Nigel Starmer-Smith's place as England scrum half. David, meanwhile, was an outstanding player at Monmouth School. Playing against the old boys' XV, his unusual ability to jink off both feet made a profound impression on the great Haydn Tanner, "I've seen the next outside half for Wales," Allan remembers Tanner saying.

The boys also enjoyed success on the cricket field, Allen recalling days playing for the Welsh schoolboys and facing up to the pace of future Test bowler David Brown, while David once claimed an analysis for Usk of four overs with four maidens and seven wickets with his off spinners. "I loved cricket but never with the same passion as rugby," he says, going on to talk of the magical Welsh players of his generation, Gareth Edwards and Barry John, who fired his enthusiasm for the game.

Elder daughter Judith travelled widely working for an American digital equipment firm but has now returned to her roots in Monmouthshire and lives just outside Abergavenny, while Jane, the youngest of the family, lives in Ipswich and works for a firm of solicitors. She and her husband, a lay preacher, are much involved with church work. Allan's children have given him seven grandchildren and, to his great delight, he is now great-grandfather to two.

Family gathering for the christening of grandchild Hannah.
David is second left, Allen third from right,
Judith next to Molly and Jane with baby Hannah.

Allan lost his beloved Molly in 2003. His loss is the greater for having depended on his wife in so many ways. "She was the one with the brains," he claims. "She looked after me and she did everything for me." Financial matters and filling in forms were always Molly's preserve. "She would even have put out the right things for him to wear," said one of his children, conscious that such matters as the choice of tie and whether he should be wearing a suit, can gnaw away at Allan as he mulls over accepting invitations to attend reunions, aware that such mundane, almost irrational, worries have always blighted his life.

Judith remembers the problems she and Molly had in persuading Allan that he would enjoy an evening at the Savoy Hotel in London when a reception was held for the post-apartheid South Africans to which those who had played against the old Springboks were invited. "I won't know anyone. No one will want to talk to me," they heard him plead, but once he found a few old chums there was no stopping him. "And when the time came to drag him away, forget it!" Judith says.

Molly and Allan: the last picture of the couple together.

It has been the same story in more recent times when his children have encouraged Allan to attend Glamorgan's former players' gatherings. He sets off wracked with doubts, but in no time he is surrounded by friends, swapping stories of old times and casting a critical eye over the shortcomings of the modern game with its noise and histrionics.

This is Allan in his element. He is seldom happier than when offering an opinion, invariably touching on some aspect how the game has changed. "I can't understand with the fast bowlers of today why they're breaking down with bad backs, bad ankles and bad knees. There must be something wrong with their actions. In my day fast bowlers were always taught to show the shoulder first. That went up and that brought the swing. But now they're coming up square on to the wicket, and they're just arming the ball.

They're not using their bodies; they can't be. And it's breaking their backs."

The ultra-competitive ethos of the commercial era disturbs him. "What do you want a third umpire for?" he asks. "It's supposed to be a wonderful game of friendship. But I wouldn't want to play it now. Because they cheat. All the shouting and they don't seem to take any notice of the umpire. Their heads go up, their arms go up and they know damn well the batsman hasn't hit the ball."

"I despair of cricket, the way it's going," he says. Yet the game that brought him so much joy can still reignite Allan's heart when he sees youngsters at practice. He is thrilled to see the nets at Oundle School opened to a wider range of less privileged children. "Something that did make the old heart beat! I went up there one Friday evening and there were hundreds of these youngsters. There were about four or five coaches and there were ladies taking coaching. Wonderful!"

Allan lives on in his Oundle home. It is as neat and tidy as when Molly was there to care for it. Neighbours keep a watchful eye on his welfare and he, in his turn, is ever ready with a helping hand, offering friends a lift into the centre of the town. The garden is one of the neatest on the estate, maintaining the tradition his father set behind the Mill Street cottage in Usk. Allan gives credit for this to his family, whose regular visits supplement the help he receives from a couple of pupils of the school sent round for an afternoon's gardening once a week. "They usually just have a cup of tea and a chat," he says of his Oundle helpers. Small wonder, for this is a man with a gift for talking and a fund of stories worth listening to.

Allan retired from first-class cricket more than 45 years ago, but he is still remembered as one the heroes of Welsh sport. At a gala dinner at the Cardiff City Hall in May 2005, with his old friend Don Shepherd and Ryder Cup golfer Brian Huggett, he was inducted into the Welsh Sports Hall of Fame. A keen follower of cricket, Huggett was thrilled to have his name linked with the two Glamorgan players. "Don has been a good friend of mine for many, many years," he said. "And Allan Watkins was one of my Glamorgan heroes when I was a little boy growing up in Neath. My mum and dad bought me an Allan Watkins bat and I handed it down to my nephew. I kept it that long."

Allan looks back on a life in which cricket has opened doors to a world far beyond the aspirations of a labourer's son from Usk. "It was a strenuous life," he admits. "But, as a youngster, it was what I had always dreamt of doing, sport, and that's what I've done. It made me take a lot of pills for being nervous, but I wouldn't change a minute."

Postscript

This book has been an attempt to place on record some of the deeds of Allan Watkins, and some of his thoughts on the game of cricket. Allan is a man of his age, happy to have played the game when he did – for all the modest rewards it brought him. "I've had a wonderful life," he says, regretting only that his chosen career so often made him an absent father when his children were growing up. He owes much to cricket, but the game is in his debt for all he has given back to it.

Perhaps, at first, he was a lucky cricketer. Few had achieved less than Allan when he won his first Test cap. Yet the scales were surely tipped against him in later years when a stronger England team could find no room for him in the mid-1950s. A man with 1,640 runs at 34.89 and 103 wickets at 15.82 in 1954 was not thought good enough to win a place in Len Hutton's team to Australia.

The nuisance value of left-hand batsmen has always helped win them selection. In the early post-war years England cast the net wide in the hope of finding a successor to Maurice Leyland or Eddie Paynter. Statistics suggest that none came closer to answering their quest than Allan Watkins. Despite his sluggish start in Tests, he ended with an average of 40.50 for his 810 runs. It is a record no other left-hand batsman chosen for England in his time can challenge. Of his contemporaries playing more than his 15 Tests all fall some way below:

	Tests	Average	100s
Ikin	18	20.89	0
Watson	23	25.85	2
Close	22	25.34	0

There were several others chosen for a handful of games – Smithson, Crapp, Dewes, Wharton, Poole and wicket-keeper Spooner, whose batting helped win him selection. There were those who came later in Allan's career, Peter Richardson and Don Smith, and those for whom places were found on major tours, Ken Suttle and Vic Wilson. Yet no left-hand batsman of the post-war years exceeded Allan's average in Tests for England until the advent of Raman Subba Row and Geoff Pullar at the end of the 1950s. Moreover, no player on the list can claim superiority as a bowler and fielder.

With the ball Allan achieved less at the highest level. The man first chosen to open the attack against Bradman's men took only 11 Test wickets, but his best years as a bowler came when his England days were over, and in Tests he never enjoyed the chance of rich pickings against weak opposition on helpful pitches.

In the end, this may be the story of a man denied his true deserts, but it has recorded the deeds of one of Glamorgan's most outstanding cricketers, and one of the good guys of cricket.

Allan at home in 2007

Acknowledgements and Bibliography

To Allan, for giving me and my tape recorder so many hours, for lending me his precious scrap book and for digging out old photographs, I shall be eternally grateful. Many others have been helpful in talking to me. I have visited Allan's brother Selwyn and his wife Eileen, Peter Walker and Donald Carr. I have spoken on the telephone with Allan's children and with others who knew him on the cricket field or at Oundle School: Tom Graveney, Leo Harrison, Michael Mills, Peter Mills, Don Shepherd, Dr Barry Trapnell and Ossie Wheatley. My thanks are extended to all.

I have made regular use of the following reference books:
Wisden Cricketers' Almanack
Playfair Cricket Annual
The Wisden Book of Obituaries (Macdonald Queen Anne Press, 1986)
Philip Bailey, Philip Thorn and Peter Wynne-Thomas, *Who's Who of Cricketers* (Second Edition) (Hamlyn Books, 1993)
Christopher Martin-Jenkins, *Who's Who of Test Cricketers* (Macdonald Queen Anne Press, 1987)
E.W.Swanton and George Plumptre (eds), *Barclays World of Cricket* (Collins, 1986)

I have consulted and sometimes quoted from:
David Rayvern Allen, *Arlott* (Harper Collins, 1994)
John Arlott, *Gone to the Cricket* (Longmans Green, 1948)
Stephen Chalke, *At the Heart of English Cricket* (Fairfield Books, 2001)
Jack Fingleton *Brightly Fades the Don* (Collins, 1949)
Andrew Hignell, *Turnbull* (Tempus, 2001)
Douglas Miller, *Born to Bowl* (Fairfield Books, 2004)
J.H.Morgan, *Glamorgan County Cricket Club* (Convoy Publications, 1952)
Gordon Ross, *The Testing Years* (Stanley Paul, 1958)
Peter Walker, *It's not just Cricket* (Fairfield Books, 2006)
Wilfred Wooller, *A History of County Cricket: Glamorgan* (Arthur Barker, 1971)

I have consulted and quoted from sundry newspapers, principally *The Times, The South Wales Echo* and *The Western Mail*, but also others, including South African and Indian papers, not readily identifiable from Allan Watkins' scrapbook.

For access to MCC minutes I am indebted to Adam Chadwick and Glenys Williams.

My principal source of statistics has been www.cricketarchive.com

I am grateful to David Jeater, series editor, and to Stephen Chalke for their encouragement and for suggested improvements to the initial script. I am grateful to Peter Griffiths for his zealous attention to detail in preparing the text for printing.

Many of the photographs used appear by kind permission of Glamorgan Cricket Archives, Eiddwen Clift, who has passed her late husband's collection to Glamorgan, and Usk Cricket Club. The photograph of Oundle School has been supplied by Tony Howorth. Other pictures come from Allan's collection or were taken by myself.

Appendix
Some Statistics

Test Cricket: Batting and Fielding

		M	I	NO	R	HS	Ave	100	50	Ct
1948	v Australia	1	2	0	2	2	1.00	-	-	-
1948/49	v SA	5	9	2	251	111	35.85	1	1	6
1949	v NZ	1	2	1	55	49*	55.00	-	-	1
1951/52	v India	5	8	1	450	137*	64.28	1	3	4
1952	v India	3	3	0	52	48	17.33	-	-	6
Career		**15**	**25**	**4**	**810**	**137***	**40.50**	**2**	**4**	**17**

Test Cricket: Bowling

		O	M	R	W	Ave
1948	v Australia	4	1	19	0	-
1948/49	v South Africa	40	4	149	4	37.25
1949	v New Zealand	3	1	11	0	-
1951/52	v India	116	26	264	4	55.00
1952	v India	51	13	111	3	37.00
Career	**6-ball**	**174**	**41**⎫	**554**	**11**	**50.36**
	8-ball	**40**	**4**⎭			

Note: Overs bowled in 1948/49 were of eight balls.

First-Class Cricket: Batting and Fielding

	M	I	NO	R	HS	Ave	100	50	Ct
1939	5	6	3	57	23*	19.00	-	-	-
1946	15	19	3	326	119	20.37	1	-	18
1947	28	47	5	1407	146	33.50	4	7	27
1948	28	46	5	1103	111*	26.90	2	3	40
1948/49	15	18	2	474	111	29.62	1	4	18
1949	30	48	4	1331	129	30.25	4	6	28
1950	29	39	7	1306	105	40.81	1	10	36
1951	33	51	5	1620	147	35.21	3	8	40
1951/52	19	25	2	872	137*	37.91	2	4	19
1952	30	49	10	1267	107	32.48	1	7	25
1953	25	35	7	1104	116	39.42	2	8	20
1953/54	7	8	1	357	90	51.00	-	3	5
1954	33	54	7	1640	170*	34.89	2	9	29
1955	31	52	4	1160	111	24.16	2	3	26
1955/56	11	15	1	256	59	18.28	-	2	10
1956	26	42	2	834	74	20.85	-	5	23
1957	27	45	6	1199	140	30.74	2	6	34
1958	28	48	5	1314	143*	30.55	1	9	21
1959	27	45	2	1330	132	30.93	3	7	24
1960	28	46	5	1077	107	26.26	1	5	15
1961	8	14	1	306	57	23.53	-	2	3
1963	1	1	0	21	21	21.00	-	-	-
Career	**484**	**753**	**87**	**20361**	**170***	**30.57**	**32**	**108**	**461**

First-Class Cricket: Bowling

	O	M	R	W	Ave	5i
1939	50	5	187	1	187.00	-
1946	8	0	57	0	-	-
1947	0	0	0	0	-	-
1948	545.2	130	1183	43	27.48	1
1948/49	96	12	352	4	88.00	-
1949	709.2	176	1799	68	26.45	-
1950	368.5	102	799	38	21.02	1
1951	678.2	177	1601	64	25.01	-
1951/52	426.2	111	969	25	38.76	-
1952	772.1	195	1890	88	21.47	2
1953	512.4	145	1265	53	23.86	2
1953/54	79.2	10	266	5	53.20	-
1954	758.3	248	1630	103	15.82	7
1955	984	270	2336	114	20.49	6
1955/56	145	62	282	7	40.28	-
1956	668.3	194	1613	58	27.81	-
1957	415.2	108	951	26	36.57	-
1958	585.3	148	1430	77	18.57	5
1959	373.5	97	921	24	38.37	-
1960	297.3	70	732	32	22.87	1
1961	45	12	104	2	52.00	-
1963	10	2	27	1	27.00	-
Career 6-b	8383.3	2257⎱	20394	833	**24.48**	25
8-b	146	17⎰				

Note: Overs bowled in 1939 and 1948/9 were of eight balls.

First-Class Cricket: Centuries

1946	119*	Glamorgan	v Surrey at Cardiff
1947	146	Glamorgan	v Northamptonshire at Kettering
	111	Glamorgan	v Worcestershire at Ebbw Vale
	105	Glamorgan	v Somerset at Weston-super-Mare
	110	Glamorgan	v Surrey at Cardiff
1948	101	Glamorgan	v Worcestershire at Worcester
	111*	Glamorgan	v South of England
1948/49	111	England	v South Africa at Johannesburg
1949	104	Glamorgan	v Surrey at The Oval
	104	Glamorgan	v Essex at Ebbw Vale
	109	Glamorgan	v Nottinghamshire at Trent Bridge
	129	Glamorgan	v Leicestershire at Swansea
1950	105	Glamorgan	v Northamptonshire at Ebbw Vale
1951	147	Glamorgan	v Kent at Swansea
	128	Glamorgan	v Sussex at Llanelli
	122	Glamorgan	v Sussex at Hastings
1951/52	137*	England	v India at Delhi
	113*	MCC	v Bengal at Calcutta
1952	107	Glamorgan	v Leicestershire at Neath
1953	114	Glamorgan	v Worcestershire at Swansea
	116	Glamorgan	v Essex at Llanelli
1954	170*	Glamorgan	v Leicestershire at Swansea
	104	Glamorgan	v Essex at Colchester
1955	111	Glamorgan	v Nottinghamshire at Llanelli
	107*	Glamorgan	v Worcestershire at Swansea
1957	115*	Glamorgan	v Sussex at Swansea
	140	Glamorgan	v Hampshire at Portsmouth
1958	143*	Glamorgan	v Northamptonshire at Northampton
1959	132	Glamorgan	v Leicestershire at Leicester
	100	Glamorgan	v Lancashire at Llanelli

	120			Glamorgan v Lancashire at Old Trafford
1960	107			Glamorgan v Leicestershire at Swansea

First-Class Cricket: Five Wickets in an Innings

	O	M	R	W	
1948	16	6	19	5	Glamorgan v Warwickshire at Neath
	19	5	40	5	Glamorgan v Northamptonshire at Kettering
1952	13.3	6	16	5	Glamorgan v Leicestershire at Neath
	19.4	6	50	7	Glamorgan v Worcestershire at Cardiff
1953	18	13	11	6	Glamorgan v Ireland at Margam
	37	10	93	5	Glamorgan v Nottinghamshire at Cardiff
1954	13	2	29	7	Glamorgan v Gloucestershire at Gloucester
	21	18	12	5	Glamorgan v Yorkshire at Neath
	27	8	54	6	Glamorgan v Somerset at Cardiff
	26	8	56	5	Glamorgan v Sussex at Swansea
	34	6	90	7	Glamorgan v Sussex at Eastbourne
	19	2	43	6	Glamorgan v Hampshire at Cardiff
	11.3	2	28	7	Glamorgan v Derbyshire at Chesterfield
1955	28	7	63	5	Glamorgan v Surrey at The Oval
	11	5	13	5	Glamorgan v Somerset at Newport
	23	6	63	5	Glamorgan v Leicestershire at Loughborough
	27.3	8	57	6	Glamorgan v Essex at Pontypridd
	38.3	13	89	5	Glamorgan v Middlesex at Cardiff
	16	5	43	5	Glamorgan v Warwickshire at Neath
1958	18.5	8	29	5	Glamorgan v Nottinghamshire at Trent Bridge
	13.2	5	19	5	Glamorgan v Derbyshire at Derby
	21	7	49	5	Glamorgan v Kent at Swansea
	28.9	4	59	5	Glamorgan v Sussex at Worthing
	17	2	52	5	Glamorgan v Lancashire at Old Trafford
1960	16	7	36	5	Glamorgan v Gloucestershire at Ebbw Vale